The First
to Escape

Clara Hsu

E T
o   R
P   Y
Hotel
Press

ISBN 978-0-9891578-7-2

Library of Congress Control Number: 2014909263

Poetry Hotel Press
P.O.Box 347063, San Francisco, CA 94134-7063
www.poetryhotelpress.com

For Jack, with gratitude.

Acknowledgements

The following poems have been previously published by:

Tower Journal: Into the Universe, From Dallas to Istanbul, Things That Are and Things That Dream, Like Cereal/Like Ceres, New Year, Tristesse.
9th Street Lab: Fughetta, Poison, Wandering Night, Lunch Talk, Tagaq Kronos.
Sparkle + Blink: Not Ethnic Enough, Metamorphosis of a Poem by Su Shi.
The Other Voices International Project: Grasp.
Erbacce Journal #33: Casa Lena, Wandering Night, ekillike, From the Beach.
I Know Something About Love: Parasol unit/Koenig Books: Chance by Xu Zhimo.
Feather Floating on the Water: My Son Likes to Get Lost in the City.
Caveat Lector: Rain.
North Coast Literary Review: Mad House Fantasia and Fugue.

Deep appreciation to Jack Foley for editing this book.

Contents

ix   Introduction by Jack Foley

xii   Author's Foreword

Not Ethnic Enough

19   Elegy to a Lost Necklace

20   Things that Are and Things that Dream

21   Rain

24   From the Beach

26   Grasp

29   From Dallas to Istanbul

31   Triptych

32   Not Ethnic Enough

36   Metamorphosis of Su Shi's "Nien Nu Jiao"

40   Tristesse

Casa Lena / and Other Place

42   Wandering Night

44   Casa Lena

45   Moving with Li Po

48   Chance Becomes Owl Inn

50   Las Momias de Quanajuato

52   Fughetta

55   Sonatine

59   ekillike

60   Cafe Delirium

62   ¿?

63   Desayuno with Oscar Wilde

65   Philosopher's Way

69   A Room in Diyarbakır

78   Tagaq Kronos

80   Into the Universe

Interlude

82   The First to Escape

90   Poison

Like Water

94   Tao-te Ching and Complications

We Shall Be Changed

105   Lunch Talk

106   The Monkey King Makes an Offering

108   backwash

109   Nit in a Faux Mink

110   SIN

112   Like Cereal / Like Ceres

114   My Son Likes to Get Lost in the City

116   The Juliad

123   We Shall Be Changed

124   E X C E L S I O R

126   Mad House Fantasia and Fugue

132   Sweet Monday

134   Reunion

136   New Year

Introduction

Though she describes herself as "not ethnic enough," everything in this book bears the brand of Clara Hsu's Chinese identity. A couplet like this,

> Where there is no beginning or end
> there are definitely walls "wars"

would have a profoundly different effect if it had been written by a non Chinese person. Those troublesome r's and l's—so often mindlessly parodied by the non Chinese—inform the words "walls" and "wars," and each of those words might suggest aspects of Chinese experience in the USA.

At the same time—as Clara generously acknowledges in her "Author's Foreword"—the work in this book has, since 2011, been decidedly influenced by a *non* Chinese consciousness: mine. On August 23, 2011, she told me that she was no longer satisfied with the work she had been doing and wished to get beyond it. But she had no idea *how* to get beyond it. "Can you," she asked me, "bring me to a break-through?" I answered yes.

If the work in this book is "experimental" in the usual sense of that word—in terms of linguistic forms—it is "experimental" in another sense as well: it is the result of an experiment in teaching that has had many consequences for both Clara and me. For the teacher and the student found themselves in a realm in which such "traditional" roles were constantly in question. If I was Clara's teacher, I was also her student. I opened various "doors"—doors that needed to be opened—but what she found on the other side of them was often material that I had no idea was there. Our teacher-student relationship became a mode of collaboration. *It was part of my teaching technique that I did not treat the student as an autonomous "individual."* I insisted that something outside the student was constantly impinging upon her—whether in the form of quotations from other writers or direct input by me. To write, it seemed to me, was not to enter the realm of "self-expression" but to enter a realm in which boundaries were continually in flux. As such, writing was the expression of *another realm of consciousness*—a realm in which self and other were constantly touching and in which the writer witnessed the dissolution of the personal "I." Language—with the deep history words bring with them—was at the center of this realm. If one's "personal" history could be present here, it was only one element in a structure in which anything was possible—In which fantasy and reality, "truth" and "fiction" danced together. Writing was fundamentally an astonishment: you wrote what you *didn't* know. The ancient word for this kind of awareness was "inspiration," by etymology a breathing in rather than an "expression"—a pressing out. I told Clara of Jack Spicer's opinion that his poetry came from "spooks" or Martians—from something other than "himself." To teach was not to impart "knowledge" so much as it was to bring the student into the realm of inspiration.

Inspiration is the lynchpin of this book. Though I make various appearances in *The First to Escape*, the book is deeply and richly Clara Hsu's. The many quotations and my occasional insertions of text are fundamentally a declaration that (to paraphrase John Donne) no one is a monad and that "the practice of outside"—Robin Blazer's phrase—is an element of all consciousness. This book demonstrates the richness and expansiveness of a poetry that recognizes that fact and swings with it. As Ezra Pound remarked about *The Cantos,* it "reminds the ready reader that we were not born yesterday."

Clara Hsu is also a professional musician, and this book clearly makes a music—a music which extends to what I believe is the *only* homophonic translation of a Chinese poem that anyone has produced. (Louis Zukofsky and David Melnick, respectively, stick to Latin and Greek; Howard L. Chace's "Frayer Jerker" is from the French.) As Eastern and Western modes harmonize and collide—and though there are autobiographical elements here—reading this book makes it clear that *you don't have to write autobiography (grandmother's congee) in order to write "ethnic" poetry.* Poems like "Not Ethnic Enough," "Moving with Li Po," "Metamorphosis of a Poem by Su Shi," and "Mad House Fantasia and Fugue"—to say nothing of the amazing sequence on the *Tao-te Ching*—reveal Hsu's Chinese identity in a way that would be impossible to the autobiographically-bound construct that is the usual "ethnic" offering. And if she plays on "walls" and "wars" in the title poem, look at what she does to the word "like" in "ekillike." Clara Hsu was born in Hong Kong; she came to the United States as a young girl. How is Hong Kong *like* San Francisco? How is she *like* American women? What does she *like* about America? (The poem began as a response to another Chinese-American woman's work—and to the woman's excessive use of "like"—but behind it is also Gertrude Stein's palindromic portrait of Lipschitz: "Like and like likely and likely likely and likely like and like.")

The range of the work and of the intellect in *The First to Escape* is extraordinary. That the book is "challenging" is no doubt true. But you will find feelings and perceptions here that you will not find anywhere else. Most importantly, you will find poetry. This Hong-Kong-born, San-Francisco-residing, Chinese-English-speaking writer/performer has an exquisite ear for the structures of American verse. Passages like this abound:

> Desolation landscape
> dissolves
> into glasses of tea.
> For every sameness, a sugar cube.
> The wind of Marmara flings specks of rain.
> Love is a dew drop on the lip.
> Night, cold, sits on the bridge.
> At the end of the fishing line, a pulse.
> "Desire goes out"
> despite sleepiness,
> "to things as they are in themselves."

Finally, there is this from Hsu's translations of the *Tao-te Ching*:

> Out of life, into death.
> Three out of ten are disciples of life.
> Three out of ten are disciples of death.
> Those who are alive, active until death,
> are also three out of ten.
> People ask why?
> Because they live on life's richness.

Jack Foley
April (Poetry Month) 2014

Author's Foreword

Each poem shall be the ripping apart of a poem. —Edith Södergran.

The majority of the poems in this collection are built upon a consciousness that did not exist two years ago. This consciousness would have remained closed had there not been an initiation. Like Dante who was led by Virgil through a tour of hell, I was taken into the universe of poets and writers, multiplicity of the mind and voices by a singular teacher—Jack Foley. He is famous for inserting his lines between other people's verses, insisting on the presence of voices within a voice. His mantra: "One part of the mind doesn't know what other parts of the mind are doing." Exploration begins when one loses one's self / identity to the fantastical variants in the real and imagined worlds. When the concept of individuality is broken down, something other than the "self" appears, and the poet steps into territories that never were before.

Poems such as "Fughetta," "Sonatine," "Mad House Fantasia and Fugue" were written specifically with classical musical forms in mind. Words become "notes" and motifs—ideas that recur, expand, build upon each other, collide, and merge. Rhythm and tempo are conveyed by space, punctuation, placement of words and phrases on the page. Expressiveness is achieved through the use of language.

Visual elements sometimes play a prominent role in determining the construction of a poem. "Philosopher's Way" has a hidden path. The upright mummies in a museum are portrayed in "Las Momia de Quanajuato." "Tagaq Kronos" is an attempt to recreate the intensity of a musical performance.

While translating a Chinese poem, a line about a young bride stirred up an image from James Joyce's *Finnegans Wake*. The result is a juxtaposition of two enchanting young girls from different times and culture. Along with lines out of Eliot's *The Waste Land*, Zukofsky's *"A"* and H.D.'s *Island*, etc., poets from the East and West dialogue in "Metamorphosis of Su Shi's Nien Nu Jiao." In another, the homophonic translation of Zu Ximo's much revered poem, "Chance," takes on a farcical tone and turns edgy, when "Chance Becomes Owl Inn."

Cubicles are not for flying objects. Form often determines the content of this collection. Although in the end, as Charles Olson wrote in his essay on *Projective Verse*, form invariably becomes "an extension of content."

To escape is to abandon—

Clara Hsu

I wait for my escape signal.
It never comes.

Not
Ethnic
Enough

Elegy to a Lost Necklace
(an octo)

Small aqua star gleamed on my throat
Held by a string of naked beads
Stunning in its simplicity
Now the bell tolls for it is lost
The one necklace I treasured most
Memory of its simplicity
Held by a string of naked beads
Small star, gleaming, in dark unknown

Elegy to a Lost Necklace / A Necklace of Words

Small aqua star gleamed on my throat
Here, take this, a necklace of words
Held by a string of naked beads
Sorrow for the lost aqua star
Stunning in its simplicity
I saw you wear it more than once
Now the bell tolls for it is lost
But beyond the fact of seeing
The one necklace I treasured most
"Things" take on our deeper being
Memory of its simplicity
I saw you wear it more than once
Held by a string of naked beads
Sorrow for the sweet aqua star
Small star, gleaming, in dark unknown
Here, take this, a necklace of words

—Clara Hsu / *Jack Foley*

Things that Are and Things that Dream

Cool air rushes in from an open window.
   The curtain fringes waver: yes/no.

Gulls cry
   like babies in distress. Such sorrow as they
   circle a slow dance above the minarets.

Inside Sinan's courtyard
   his handprints heavy on each ancient brick.

Shape of a tulip
   a young girl with headscarf, her long waist leaning
for a butterfly kiss.

The half moon
   separates things that are from things that dream
   holds them upon her face.

The cobblestone street
   whoever walked here today has appeared and disappeared.

Earlier on, an orange cat put his paws on my knees.
   You said it is in search of love.
   I said it is lonely.

Things that are
have no need for us.

Things that dream
are what we're made of.

Rain

The bed, a womb
every night a returning.
Slip into
and under
way, unseen, unknown.

Into the ears pours
a tipped jar of marbles.

The hemisphere fissures.
Along the beak lines
rain—
little hands turn frantic,
tapping, "Open, open,
pip pang patty-cake!"

"What did you say?"
across a continent of static
the possibility is that
she has been repeating, "I love you."

I
  lo
    u
         le-o
fff
  ev-   ol

  lv-eo

And he's thinking of

those **U**s

curve**S**

his **t**ongue **l**icks the air

the moist air, saturated, swollen—
that may burst open at any time
and come down with a grunt.

Suddenly it's not busy anymore.

Brilliant darkness.

Only the sound of feet splashing in
puddles
comes from all directions
and the giggles of a young girl:

> *Oriolopos chimera-*
> *hunter of white morning—*
> *measly.*
> *Dramdrinker meets La Belle Sauvage—*
> *thunderbolt!*

Yellow dog chases
teal snake races
calico cat tangled with
ribbons and laces
when the blue sky rages
they fear the mages.

mirsu falls.

                              (singing)
She rises after the rain
ribbons arching over clouds
born to the sun and water nymph
iridescent in her grace.

She dips her luminous hands
breaks up the hypothesis of the eye
like the dust on a butterfly's wing
like Argus' sinister spies.

She evanesces under nature's brush
leaves as quiet as she comes
leaves the sea to its howling
blends trees with mountain mist.

(End singing)

When he paints her
she pretends to be asleep.
When he finishes she is truly
asleep, and he finds himself
unwanted.

naif falls.

The languid fog
hurries a man
along a half dark street
walks fast to get away from
the stinging mist
but slow to go home to
a sullen wife,
and children drugged
in front of video game screens.
It makes him wonder

toothless is the moon
when the crescent is its face.

"Which gate do you come from
and from which one do you leave?"

a new born
cries from
the shadow
of a column

"Miserable rain."

Note: Words in italics are taken from James Joyce's *Finnegans Wake*.

From the Beach

Sea voices
> *Sea voices*

freighter on the horizon
> *freighter on the horizon*

a bench
> *a bench*

A girl lifts her wings
> *a girl lifts her wings*
standing on a ledge.
> *standing on a ledge.*
The next gust
> *The next gust*
takes her into the ocean
> *takes her into the ocean*
her dress billowing.
> *her dress billowing.*

It's overcast.
> *It's overcast.*
The beach is sleepy.
> *The beach is sleepy.*
We disappear
> *We disappear*
down
> *down*
a straight long path
> *a straight long path*
misted
> *misted*
in
> *in*
fog.
> *fog.*

My hair
      Your hair
in your mouth
      in my mouth
your eyes
      your eyes
darkening
      darkening
the sun
      the sun

sand and salt.
      sand and salt.

Grasp

I leave
to another there
and here.

Is it Prague,
stilted grim faces bleeding with history;
or Assos,
sunning by the Aegean,
saffron and paprika colorings
that I am acquainted with stones?

Or is it in my bedroom,
where an egg-shaped
likeness of a Buddha happens in my palm?

The other day
the white stone on railing
rests a butterfly.

All these,
I heed.

The unspeaking pieces
gather me.

◆

This morning my urge to draw you deepens
when rusty fingers call for purpose.

In our room there're books and stones
and things practicing stillness for months
or maybe years, wearing powder and silk,
the layers of time.
Shades lighten
on your graying chest

where I place a paper.
One hand feeling your torso
the other sketches.

Unstirred in your nakedness
you clothe me with tedium,
and I
waken
cover your thighs.

Rise to make tea,
boil water a hundred times;
we made love a thousand times somewhere.
Now cool to touch,
it is late afternoon before I drink.
Long, shiny leaves resting abundant
in amber liquid.

Bitter.

◆

The church bells in the city
where we bed clang
with neuroses.
We lapse into oblivion
licking the salt on our lips.

My nipples,
hard like the statues on Charles Bridge,
yearn for the sun to set.

Bodies converge
after glasses of mint tea,
intone to donkey carts and motor cycles.
Remnants of gratitude
emerge in deserts,
citadels,
towns where streets are filled with pot holes,

trains with depressing men,
camps of bones, house of death.

In the old Jewish cemetery
bodies are piled twelve layers deep.
Stones upon stones, mangled roots,
dry leaves a firework of lunacy,
massively dishevelled,
intuit darkness.

◆

Strange the winter sun smears
a print on silver sea sky.
My yearning for you
is strong as for a man.
Your debilitation a sacred blossom.
It is delicacy I worship.
Like gulls gliding over water for fish,
I wish to plunge into your afflictions.
When each moment disperses into infinite spores,
timeless, not time
I spend with you.

From Dallas To Istanbul

"Boarding First Class Passengers."
  Will the elite please be seated.
    "Don't you know me by now? I really don't care."

Boy bouncing up and down on the automatic walkway.
  Starbucks' Earl Gray. Gulp it down. Tall, Grande, Venti, whatever—
lifestyle sophistication—they mean.
    "Turkish tea, apple tea, Nescafe?"

Line forming. Into the tunnel of no return.
  All we like sheep, have (not) gone astray...husbands, wives,
friends, lovers, businessmen, doctors, lawyers, architects, contractors,
teachers, musicians, artists, babies. POET.
    "People!"

Old man with breasts. Backpack, shorts, tennis shoes.
  My father's breasts are naturally aged.
    "My hands on yours..."

Beep. You passed. Beep. Beep.
  How many affairs do you need? Who's keeping scores?
Have I passed? Am I a poet now?
    "Get a life, you say?"

The corridor is strangely quiet.
  Like the heart. It knows.
    "I knew from the moment I set eyes on you."

Caution. Slippery when wet.
  Words.
    "Voices!"

Oneworld.
  One. The body is an extension of the mind and it is beautiful.
    "I love you I love you I..."

The stewardess cannot (will not) help you with your luggage.

Suddenly there are two worlds. Us vs. them.

"We cannot get rid of the people around us, those boring, dull people who rob us of the pleasures of life."

"Did you order a special meal?" she asked, coldly.

What about drugs? Never tried, though got high on second hand pot smoke once.

My daughter's boyfriend told me to eat some psychedelic mushrooms. A few bites would take me into the altered state.

"Yumm. More...you."

"Fasten your seatbelt," the machine said. It's all machine from Dallas to Istanbul.

Peter, we must meet up after your session with Hilary Clinton. I understand. Work first. But S.F.—D.C.—IST! What synchronistic serendipity!

"And we must get used to not being together." signed, me.

Triptych

Kisses
He kisses me on the lips.
He tongue-kissed me.
We kissed.

"I dreamt of you
kissing someone else," he says.

He tongue-kissed me.
We kissed.
He looks on.
"I dreamt of
making love to you," he says,
and pecks me on the cheek.

Winter Seed
There's no light
because
she doesn't believe
in the light

deep freeze

Morning
Only a slither of sun   until the insistent sun.
peeks through closed curtains.
A truck growls, turning the corner.
        A moan grows, inside the house.
The books with all their eloquence
hold their peace.
Only the fingers, purposeful,
lift the first veil, trace
the roundness of the fruits
before paring down to the skin
to regard, to caress, to squeeze, to taste,
to desire, to kiss, to tease,
to love, to memorize, to recall,
to kiss, to let go,
and kiss
and let go.

Not Ethnic Enough

Like a charm on a red string, for protection
     those cards
               throw them
    on the table.
King of Hearts,
Queen of Diamonds,
all wearing glasses.

The jester: Where's my coffee?   Turkish tea cups
  green tea is so much better.   Made in China
  Ph balanced · antioxidant ·   Made in China
  trace minerals · greater   Made in China
    longevity · lower   You, Chine?
    mortality   Evet! Made in China!

Chinatown is changing subtly. The men sitting in the bakery drinking coffee and buying
lottery tickets will gradually fade away, so will the homemade basement temples, and the
old gangsters who talk football at one o'clock in the morning at Sam Wo.

The old man chews on a toothpick   "My father is old but his
while reading the Sing-Tao Daily news.   mind is very young."
Undershirt · toenails · teeth · yellowing

                 I'm young but feeling…

        "…Sefu…Sefu!"
Master Po, King Lear of the milky eyes
your name is Keye Luke · (Luke Sek Lam) ·
               Kwai Chang Caine · Shaolin monk · three in one ·
               David Carradine · Keith Carradine · Radames Pera
Charlie Chan is the Swedish
Warner Oland · (Johan Verner Ölund) ·
               Kato, valet to the Green Hornet
               Bruce Lee · (Lee Yun-fan · Lee Xiao-lung) ·

      This tree is questionable as to
         who's what ·
       who's who ·
       who's not ·

Waverly, you need something to call home.

In the middle of the night
an aspen quakes,
"Go down," a voice coaxes,
"only those tentacles that hold the earth are real."

> But you swing on the branches
> and watch the moon hurtling down
> and up, a revolving crystal ball
> eluding your grasp…

The Wong Benevolent Association on Waverly Place
decks out its flags. "No parking" signs are tied onto
the lamp posts between Sacramento and Clay. A row
of folding chairs is set up in front of the building. A
man with a rag wipes down the red plastic seats and
rusty frames. Old folks, done up, pin big ribbon rosettes
on their chests.

> "The magic of light encased, swinging on a long stick,
> flickering. The glimmer inside a paper fish's belly,
> yellow star fruit, hairy rambutan. When I was small I
> pulled a little white curly crepe rabbit with four wooden
> wheels. A candle was lit inside, held by a thin wire. My
> sister and I walked up and down the length of the short
> corridor at home. She held a butterfly of transparent
> wings. We were the keepers of light, short legs toddling,
> gleeful and drooling, a kind of mythical youngling along
> with the shadows that were cast on the walls and ceiling."

"You'd better know all the numbers before going in."
　"I think I'm missing the number gene."

> "In a five syllabic finite poem expressiveness
> is to be derived only from the varied tone of
> each character."

sometimes
when I
breathe
　·
the
cold air
jolts
me
that the right vocabulary · ethnic · minority · crisis · is necessary in order to go places. That

these · empowerment · possibility · equality · buzz words justify value and lead to general consent · tradition · culture · roots · preservation · of an existence. That a few words · race · discrimination · sexism · may explain all the problems of the Now. That the brown indelible skin is a ticket to · rave · rant · rage ·

My eyes?	not ethnic enough
My hair?	not ethnic enough
My accent?	not ethnic enough
My grandfather?	not ethnic enough
My grandmother?	not ethnic enough
My origin?	not ethnic enough
	if those words
	are absent

folds of the sun
> *the sun folds, gives up*

folds of moth wings
> *the moth flies into the sun*

folds of the blue-tongue fire
> *my tongue touching yours, sweetly, a "fire"*

folds of the sand
> *sand and*

folds of wind clouds
> *clouds my mind*

folds of a dry sky lightning
> *the fly cries in the dry sky*

folds on a new born
> *he said "I wish to be in your 'bourn'"*

folds of crow's feet
> *get out of here, old man, let a young woman in*

folds on an old photograph
> *"stills"—as opposed to movies (someday all " photographs" will be movies)*

folds and folds of lace ribbons
> *decorating his undershorts—she saw as he removed them*

a shirt, half fold
> *UNfold*

a sock unfold
> *REfold*

folds on the arm-
> *gold folds*

chair resting
> *watch out! The chair is moving!*

The taxi driver took one look and predicted "foreigner"—the clothes, the posture —he was right every time.

"They hate me because I don't speak Chinese."

"They hate you more when you don't even try."

The illegal act my father committed was unmentionable in the 1960's. He took the train from Hong Kong to China and stayed there overnight. When he came back I tried to sniff the purported fragrance from his clothes. Not a trace could be detected. Years later when I went to Guangzhou I specifically asked to be taken to such a place, where at the show window the merchandise was lined up in a row, their bodies shiny (already cooked I suppose), hung by the necks, oil dripping down the long singed tails. They put the slices in a clay pot with daikon radishes and carrots, sizzling hot. Red meat, chewy, but it didn't taste like chicken.

"*Dog…what's the big deal?*" I asked my friend, "It's not what it's trumped up to be."

He shrugged, "People are into wild vegetables these days."

After all,
we have something in common
doggedly pursuing
afraid to die
before the body gives in.

The malaise
of a calm night
a lone street lamp bathes
in its yellow pool.
The sign in the bus shelter
scrolls a long message:
"Eternity arrives in 56 minutes."

Note: the sun folds, gives up… italicized lines by Jack Foley.

Metamorphosis of Su Shi's "Nien Nu Jiao"

Su Shi (1036-1101) was a Chinese poet of the Sung Dynasty. In this poem, the poet toured Red Cliff, site of a great sea battle that took place during the time of the Three Kingdoms (169-280). General Chou Kung-Chin used fire to destroy his opponent's chained boats, winning a decisive battle. Siu-Ch'iao was Chou's wife, famous for her beauty.

                                    Big river rushes east
           What's   The river sweats
                 left   *toward waves edge*
                     of   Oil and tar.
                          the   *millennia of romance.*
                 ebb   Today I gather all red flowers
                                                Shed their petals on the paths,
                 tide   Shimaunu-San, in the dawn—
                          West of ruins
                            people say,
                        "Three Kingdoms, Chou's Red Cliff."
           obscure   The barges drift
                 is   With the turning tide
              the   Red sails
           stain   Wide
                                   To leeward, swing on the heavy spar…
                 Jagged rocks crack clouds
                            In my garden,
                 fierce surges break banks
                     roll up heaps of snow
       Eyes   In my garden
             see   the winds have beaten
                 only   the ripe lilies;
                     this   and the salt has crept
                           far   under the leaves of the white hyacinth.
                 Pictured landscape
                 how heroes come and go.

       Mind   *Think of Kung-Chin, those years*
       the   *(Siu-Ch'iao, just married)*

changing   She was just a young thin pale soft shy slim
wind   slip of a thing then, sauntering, by silvamoonlake…
                    stunningly poised
                feathered fan and kerchief
                    between laughs
Megavolt!

                lie captives, ash and dust.

the   *Mind tours old world*
tendril   *sentiment mocks my*
of   *early gray hair.*
longing   and indeed there will be time
blown   to wonder,
  to   *Life is a dream*.
   p   "Do I dare?" and, "Do I dare?"
   i   I offer to love's play
   e   My dark declivities.
   c   *A toast to river-moon.*
   e   And, night approaching like the entrance of a tunnel,
   s   We would turn back and cannot, we
                Surprise our natures; the woods lock us up
                In the secret crimes of our intent.

Man must love and be loved,
To walk slowly in the full sympathy of noon
Is as good as beholding two trees
Leaning into one another their leaves.

O happiness! You have descended on me like a cloud!
As a bird falls silent after a well-sung day,
I shall be silent now.
Speech beyond speech—that is more to me
Than the "morn-dew" to the myrtle leaf,

Sacred to me this temporary solution
Said I.
Opposing the memory-effacing waters of Lethe
Said they.

Big River rushes east	大江東去，
toward waves edge	浪淘盡，
millennia of romance.	千古風流人物。
West of ruins	古壘西邊，
people say,	人道是，
"Three Kingdoms, Chou's Red Cliff."	三國周郎赤壁；
Jagged rocks crack clouds	亂石崩雲，
fierce surges break banks	驚濤裂岸，
roll up heaps of snow.	捲起千堆雪；
Pictured landscape	江山如畫，
how heroes come and go.	一時多少豪傑。
Think of Kung-Chin, those years	遙想公瑾當年，
(Siu-Ch'iao, just married)	小喬初嫁了，
stunningly poised	雄姿英發；
feathered fan and kerchief	羽扇綸巾，
between laughs	談笑間，
lie captives, ash and dust.	強虜灰飛煙滅。
Mind tours old world	故國神遊，
sentiment mocks my	多情應笑我，
early gray hair.	早生華髮，
Life is a dream.	人生如夢，
A toast to river-moon.	一樽還酹江月。

EPILOGUE
As she sings...

Darkling,
Darling,

*

Shadows

*

Meadows
Of
Childhood

*

Umbriago!
Dark one!

*

CLARA'S SCARF

I am like
a river moving round
and round
a countryside

Quotes:
"Today I gather…" Louis Zukofsky, *A.*
"The river sweats…" T.S. Eliot, "The Waste Land."
"In my garden…" H.D., "Island. VI."
"She was just a young…" James Joyce, *Finnegans Wake.*
"and indeed there will be time…'Do I dare?'" T.S. Eliot, "The Love Song of J. Alfred Prufrock."
"I offer to love's play…" W.B. Yeats, "A Woman Young and Old."
"And, night…" Jean Garrigue, "Forest."
"Man must love..." Jean Garrigue, "Free-Floating Report."
"EPILOGUE…" Jack Foley.

Note: a performance of the poem can be found on Youtube.com:
https://www.youtube.com/watch?v=p0DwxaBersw

Tristesse

evening, and the sadness

> *midnight, a turning*

of saturday (shadowday)

> *from one thing to another*

small failures in the walls (sudden

> *the cobwebs*

cracks that weren't there before—

> *sticky and long*

shadows that fall

> *dangle*

across—)

> *in*

space:

> *a corner*

a turning

from one thing to another—

> *missing*

your face

> *its hunger*

burning

—Jack Foley/*Clara Hsu*

Casa
Lena
&
Other
Places

Wandering Night

Begin with sadness that permeates
since the feverish hands cooled
Looking beyond
it must have been the wind
first it fanned the flames
then it sucked away the heat
leaving chalky remnants of rectangles
squares, circles of certainty.

A phallic stone • a quest of polka-dot feather
A blossom wakes • cicadas chant a mantra
Pale filigrees uncoil • under the mingled stars
Its seven white veils • stirring in the thick of night.

Are you mad?
AREYOUMAD
you babbling brook
coming down with a case of lunar spasm
frothing at the brink of your lips
the white of your eyes
grand mal, mother
loves you, dear
dear, mother
loves you.

Azul is the color • deep in an ink well
southern breeze • she prefers to call it
noir, peeling a corner • his fingers fumble
a touch of slick • a tuck in the groin

Turning
the owl's eyes widen
from its own musing
What of the scurrying mice
and beating wings in a nearby bush?
Pity the prey

ecstasy on borrowed time
one lifting talon away.

Coming into…

the dreamer
doesn't know it is she who commands
the dream to appear. It is she who has
been wishing. It is she whose wish takes
form tapping a code into the great
unknown. It is her words: I want. It is
her pining that draws the creature forward
draws it into her vicinity but she is puzzled
by its incongruous appearance. Not knowing
what to make of the dream she lets it nibble
first her ears then her eyes and nose and mouth.
She lets it kiss her mouth. She lets it touch her
face and arms she lets it consume her.

When she wakes she'll know it is she who has
asked for salvation and each time it is given
to her like a ripened fruit ready to be plucked.
It is she whose magnetic eyes reel in a new
reality and she must endure the newness
and the strangeness of it. It is in dream
that she finds. It is in dream that they
come. It is in dream that she finds them all.

Darkness disperses • like crushed little bones

Casa Lena

Remember when you were a tree?
      I do...arms, heaviness, blear peace.   Jack Kerouac

B e a u t i f u l
                f
                o
   periwinkle   r
                m
                s
the concept of a house.   h   about
                  s
Apollo's sons   a
            d
in the breeze
their owl heads spin
from dawn to dust.

Serene is the Virgin
          her splendid robe
            hung
            on a
            wall
rivers of emotion
c
 a
  s
   c
    a
    d
     i   Morning incense
      n   fair hills in a distance
      g   steeples and bells.
                         Dull noon washes
              Rain   in a sink of sunflowers.
   ¿ No   in
estoy yo aqui,   the   Fluttering wings
que soy tu Madre?   middle   take the evening down
              of   lampara de estrellas
              the   a new universe.
              night.

Moving with Li Po

Still
moving
through neglected years
Not a word—not one Chinese word!
Buried, that sentiment
of spring flower and autumn moon
cotton clouds on dark green sea.
Yellow hibiscus, the shaded shore,
pebbles, shells and large brown kelps.
Salt made lips full,
turned girls into dreamers.
Letters, blue on the desk
pressed with the reddest flame
poems in childish calligraphy.

      Li Po at Squaw Valley
      amid a roomful of American poets
           床前明月光   *Moonlight casts on bed*
      his voice, now feminine
           疑是地上霜   *bemused as ground frost*
      quivered in the act of remembering
           舉頭望明月   *Head tilt to bright moon*
      the first seed, sown in a singsong manner
           低頭思故鄉   *bow to homeward thoughts*

black coffee now
rice wine
peyote
SHROOMS

after years of abuse	花間一壺酒	*Drinking amid flowers*
the liver is failing	獨酌無相親	*alone with no friends.*
running leaves and newspapers	舉杯邀明月	*Raise cup, invite moon*
swishing cars	對影成三人	*my shadow makes three.*
each step leading to a lesser known place	月既不解飲	*Moon's dim about wine.*
does the light fall in front or behind a window	影徒隨我身	*Shadow follows me.*
that mad moon	暫伴月將影	*Now moon and shadow*
staring	行樂須及春	*frolic in the spring.*
If you should die now	我歌月徘徊	*I sing, moon lingers.*
I shall take off my clothes and begin walking	我舞影零亂	*I dance, shadow splits.*

I shall be a different animal	醒時同交歡	*Make love when we're awake.*
with unmistakable markings	醉後各分散	*Break up when we're spent.*
I shall hold the moon between my teeth	永結無情遊	*Ever zestless friends,*
and crack it like a wafer	相期邈雲漢	*meet in starry band.*

Summer of 2006. Cafe La Boheme. We sat around the table translating Li Po. Behind us the Mexicans were playing chess. R had been noticing us for some weeks. Finally he walked over and introduced himself—a German immigrant who spoke perfect Spanish. "Will you be here again next week?" he asked. "No, this is our last session."

deep yearnings	長相思
in Ch'ang-an	在長安

autumn crickets call	絡緯秋啼
at the rim of golden well	金井闌
dewy frost, mattress pale and cold	微霜淒淒簟色寒
unlit lamp brings thoughts of death	孤燈不明思欲絕
curtain furls, futile moan at moon	卷帷望月空長歎
you, a flower beyond cloud's edge	美人如花隔雲端
above, lies the blue unknown	上有青冥之長天
below, clear water rushes and whirls	下有淥水之波瀾
painful thoughts roam long and far	天長路遠魂飛苦
powerless to cross the mountain pass	夢魂不到關山難

deep yearnings	長相思
crush my heart	摧心肝

moving

the moon

Li Po

Frank Samperi

Clara

Mun-Wai

日色已盡花含煙	moon	skyscrapers
月明欲素愁不眠	moon	branches
趙瑟初停鳳凰柱		
蜀琴欲奏鴛鴦絃	blocked	
此曲有意無人傳		
願隨春風寄燕然		
憶君迢迢隔青天	blue everywhere	

昔日橫波目

今成流淚泉

不信妾腸斷

歸來看取明鏡前

light ever

center

unseen

where yes

Flowers at dusk sip smoky mist,

sleepless under a pale lit moon.

Zither rests by the Phoenix post

lute strings yearning to be strummed.

This song finds no messenger

rises with spring breeze, swallow's flight.

Thoughts of you beyond the blue sky,

then with flirting glance

now a tearful spring.

If you doubt my wretched state,

in front of my mirror, come!

clearly

flower

not unlike

no

gardens

streets

not wretched

state

projected

discoloring

sit in a park

otherworldly

Notes:

"Moonlight cast on bed…"—"Night Thought" by Li Po.

"Drinking amid flowers…"—"Drinking Along Under the Moon" by Li Po.

"Deep yearnings…" and "Flowers at dusk…"—"Deep Yearnings" by Li Po.

"Moon Skyscraper…" Excerpt from Frank Samperi's *Anamnesis*.

Chance Becomes Owl Inn

A conventional translation, a homophonic translation and an improvisation
on the poem "Chance" by Xu Zhimo.

偶然

我是天空里的一片云
偶尔投影在你的波心
你不必讶异
更无须欢喜
在转瞬间消灭了踪影
你我相逢在黑夜的海上
你有你的
我有我的方向
你记得也好
最好你忘掉
在这交会时互放的光芒。

Chance

I am a cloud in the sky
by chance it casts a shadow in your heart
don't be surprised
or happy
in an instant it all vanishes.
We meet, at sea, in the night
traveling in different directions.
You may recall
or perhaps it is better to forget
the glow when we cross paths.

◆

Owl Inn

All's tin only. Dig. Un-pinion!
Oh ewe tolling joy. Nay, dig bosom!
Nay butt, be artsy.
Gang mohr shirk fun hay.

Joy jew-shirt can seal mini toning.
Nay, all shendful jihad yet dehull sun.
Nay, you (nee Dig),
oy y'all dig for urn.
Nay gay duck yellow,
drainhole neigh modal.
Joy Gawain see wool founding Golan.

◆

Peripeteia

All's tin only. Dig. Un-pinion!
Barren.
Oh ewe tolling joy. Nay, dig bosom!
Mary Magdalene munches
Nay butt, be artsy.
a MacDonald's hamburger.
Gang mohr shirk fun hay.
Rosanne Barr is on.
Joy jew-shirt can seal mini toning.
Laughter!
Nay, all shendful jihad yet dehull sun.
"Jesus Christ,
Nay, you (nee Dig),
twenty-million tweeters..."
oy y'all dig for urn.
She licks her wrist
Nay gay duck yellow,
Ketchup dripping.
drainhole neigh modal.
Her fingers curl
Joy Gawain see wool founding Golan.
between her thighs.

Las Momias de Quanajuato

```
M        T    C                                                    O
o        h    u   d                                                n
m        e    r   r                                                e
m             l       Girls dressed as angels boys as saints
y        C    y   e                                                o
         h        d                                                u
         i            Instead of going to heaven                   t
h        n    p       Their bodies dried in arid crypts
a    L   e    u   s                                                o
s    i   s    b   a                                                f
     t   e    i   c          Now they lie behind glass cases
a    t        c   k      Sunken eyes and hollowed faces            a
     l   w        s
s    e   e    Their                                                h
l        a    a   bodies dried in arid crypts                      u
a    b   r    i   u                                                n
s    a   s    r   s                                                d
h    b            Instead of going to heaven                       r
     y   a    o   y                                                e
o        n    n                                                    d
n    b                Saints and angels in soiled laces
     y   o    b   k                                                h
h        r    u   i                                                a
e    h   i    r   n                                                s
r    e   e    l
     r   n    y   j                                                p
t        t    a   a          Tragedies:                            e
u    s   a    m   w          Man was pierced at the thorax.        r
m    i   l    a   s                 ✚                              f
m    d        n       Woman with arms over her eyes                e
y    e   d    ,   d       was mistakenly buried.                   c
.    .   r        r                 ✚                              t
         e        o   Drowning caused black and blue
         s        p       marks on a man's skin.                   s
         s        p                                                k
         .        e                                                i
                  d                                                n
                  .                                                n
                                                                   o
              "Buenas tardes," chimed the Mexican school children.
                                                                 hOle
```

Note:
Las Momias de Quanajuato is a mummy museum in Quanajuato, Mexico. Many of the mummies are displayed in upright position. While guide books warn about the grotesqueness of the mummies, it is a field-trip destination for Mexican school children.

He:

the light in your eyes
as we lay

naked

meant more to me
than any

praise

She:

your touch
is praise

each time

a quickening

Fughetta

To grasp the thread
is to follow the leaf of a very old tree
To grasp the thread
slip-sailing in a gust of wind
is to follow the leaf of a very old tree
its palm lines, the path into a forest, vast and deep.
To-grasp-the-thread-is-to-follow-the-leaf TO GRASP
of-a-very-old-tree, THE THREAD *slip-sailing in a gust of wind*
IS TO FOLLOW *its palm lines, the path* THE LEAF
into a forest, vast and deep. OF the leaf A VERY leaf OLD TREE
slip-sailing slip - sailing slip-sailing
in-
a-gust-of-wind slip-sailing slip
its-palm-lines SLIP-SAILING palm lines
INTO the-path-into A   -forest-vast-and-deep. FOREST
VAST   AND   DEEP.

Time
and its meaning
Its palm line, the path
are forgotten.
are forgotten, falters
falters
mum
between moon tease
and shadows
mum
mum
in the presence
the presence
of night
night

the light
night
vast
and
deep
your eyes
light
in the forest
as we lay
your touch
palm lines
naked
in a gust
is praise
meant more to me
each time
to me
praise
than any
praise
each time
a quickening

He:
The thread is the light
in your eyes

is to follow
as we lay
naked under   a very old tree
The thread   meant more to me
slip-sails in a gust of wind
THE THREAD IS LIGHT
is to follow the leaf   the thread
meant more
its palm lines, meant more to me than any praise
as we lay, naked   the thread is light
She:
in a forest, vast and deep
your touch
its palm lines, is praise
THE   THREAD   each time   IS LIGHT   a quickening, praise
To grasp the thread
the light in your eyes is to follow the leaf
To-grasp- *as we lay* the-thread
of a very old tree   *naked* slip-sailing   *To grasp the thread*
meant more to me   in a gust of wind   is-to-follow-the-leaf
of-a-very-old TO -tree GRASP *than any praise.*
its palm lines slip-sailing-in-a-gust-of-wind   THE   THREAD
Your touch is praise   the path into a forest IS   TO   FOLLOW   each time
THE LEAF OF *is to follow the leaf* a-quickening
A VERY   Its palm line, OLD TREE
your praise
a-path-into-the-forest
meant more than any praise
to me.

Sonatine

Agitato

filthy fingers white trash
a plastic bag of leftover   scavenger
 thin beard blond curls   At
He could be a full grown Adonis   spins   the
  an unsteady pirouette   bus
  howls arms raised *Raaaaaaahhhh*   shelter
the man wants to sit down   but there are all these girls
                    waiting

He
swings the plastic bag
above his head.
      Out flies a fork   squirt
         and a   of black
                 beans.
Filthy fingers
     nearly touching a girl's face.
       She moves.
          They all move,
"OUT!" He salutes them,
     "Hello Kitty."

        Girls would want to date
        a full grown Adonis.
        Girls would want to kiss,
        own,
        would want to… they escape into
              the open bus door
               pressing body
                against body.

     A phone message:
     "I'm sorry. The young man you sold
     the violin to is my son. Brian doesn't know
     what he is doing. May I return the instrument?"
He loiters about the neighborhood
sometimes bashful.
His mother, apologetic   He pays them no heed.
where ever he goes/she goes.   His fingers long and filthy.

Lento

This song has to do with vicissitude.
The pink of the lilies paling on stems
the cast of raccoons
sunning in a wilted garden
an old man considers the pain
on his back—

Why wings now
when the bird's-eye view
passes like a silent movie
not one is saved
   sometimes it weeps.

I have already flown
   Boys watch their friends die
albeit hovering over the edge of storms.
   as if they ought to.
Neither a hero nor villain
just a seed traveling.

The sweetness of peanut butter cookies
   Animals breed and kill
set afire
   insects feed and sting
in Memory's cavity.
   I too, am capable of

                                                              sky

       slipping   *vacuous*
         into   *a*
             silence   *toward*

Rondo

"We run a business, *business*, ma'am, all sales are final."
What day of the week is this? *What day of the week?*
The scene looks strangely familiar. She is waiting at
the piano with pencil and eraser. I haven't practiced
haven't practiced.
"Get off me, get off me, OFF,!"
Another baby? Lying on the hospital bed,
they said, "PUSH."
 "What to do? *What to do?*"
PUSH!
Give me. Give me.
"Why did you do this to me?
Why? Why?"
"All I have to say is,
you are well, he is well, she is well."

The Certains rule the Uncertains.
The Uncertains are certain
of their uncertainty
but not so certain
that they are completely uncertain.

The Certains
manipulate
the Uncertains
into thinking that they have freedom.
Certainly, all the Certains have to do
is to make the Uncertains feel certain
about THEIR position and leave
the uncertainty to whatever
the Certains oppose.

The repetition is beginning to sound like a tick.

Notes:
"Hello Kitty" is a fictional character portrayed as a female white Japanese bobtail cat with a red bow.
http://en.wikipedia.org/wiki/Hello_Kitty
Nicolas Slonimsky's "Grandmother Chord."—using all twelve tones and eleven intervals, no repeat.
http://en.wikipedia.org/wiki/Grandmother_chord#Grandmother_chord

"Water"
Ancient Chinese emblem.

ekillike

e kil is like illi
ek illi illi ke ke

e eats, like egret one foot illi illi the water flows
ek, it calls   ek   ek
no ill   like all is perfect

          the cloud
the sky   the water
               the air
as if all ills are killed   illiilli

          as if   is like
like   ekil   kile
is "tickle" in Norwegian

a figure being tickled Kekekeke

illi illi the egret wades illi illi

          as if ekil is like

Cafe Delirium

It is always better, that 'other' world
where each motion is a still frame
perfectly all right to linger in.
Forest branching
limbs-like, soft labyrinthine
brain, the maiden's hair
a sprinkle of light reflecting.
Eyes, dark rounds of intelligence
hidden, revealed, luring.
                I paint not you but what I crave
Shapes in the armchair doubled over each other
dull
with laughter
in the foamy, luscious, desirous whipped-swirls.
        Have a good sip.
                        After the rain
                        there is no more talk of rain
                        After the sun
                        there is always moon
                        After the storm and its devastation
                        there is not much
                        to talk about
                        This morning
                        your eyes stared at mine
                        After the years
                        there was no more talk
                        of love
                        After the love
                        there was no more
                        She said marriage
                        takes us into a higher plane
                        We raised our glasses
                        and went to bed
                        After the night
                        with eyes cold like neglected coffee
                        burning—
                        the outside air.
The coming and going of customers,
the good-natured barista,

the grinder, the steam, the dishes, forks, knives and spoons,
cash register, the clock that brings the hour to an end,
the nothingness that is taken/not taken away.

    Astonish me, love, or I'll break down and weep.

¿?

¿
Does
The author is unable
the
to rouse the audience
body
with her orgy story
listen
penis, breast and pubic hair
to
even the infidelity
the
lacks luster.
mind
Too many facelifts
and
but her gown
the
has a shimmering quality.
mind
She speaks politely
to
and everyone
the
claps.
body
?

¿
Can
Pumpkin seeds and beans
love
rice and corns
not
the season of harvest
be
Mariachi bands
killed
in the cemetery
and
the priest says a prayer
dead
pan de muerto
love
sweet bread
be
for the dead
regenerated
?

¿
Is
Ghost pass through the holes
the
in color-paper cuttings
soul
strung high like flags
our
across the jardin.
imagination
At the fiesta
or
church bells bend back and forth
is
people in costumes and painted faces
imagination
Diego Rivera, Salvador Dali,
the
Frida Kahlo, forever.
soul
?

Desayuno with Oscar Wilde

There is something in your voice that is wonderful.
Come, Oscar,
the past two nights you snuggled
in my bed until well past midnight.
The day is warm.
Let us follow that man
who just came out of the butcher shop,
sombrero and cane,
carrying a plastic bag of ground beef.
The aim of art is simply to create a mood.
I want to walk up calle del Pueblito,
the small street I came upon yesterday,
to have breakfast in the cactus filled courtyard.
They said Obama won the election last night.
I`m glad women won`t have to worry
about wearing iron underpants.
A little secret?
I didn´t vote this time.
The intellect of the race is wasted
in the sordid and stupid quarrels
of second-rate politicians.
There is a grotesque horror about its comedies,
and its tragedies seem to culminate in farce.
Yes, they turned my stomach
and there`s little hope
one way or another.
But look what spreads before us!
Thick rind homemade marmalade,
toasted bread, smooth dark coffee,
scrambled eggs and refried beans.
Even for us, there is left
some loveliness of environment...
"¿Jugo de naranja o zanahoria?"
I choose zanahoria because I don`t know what it is.
How fond women are of doing dangerous things.
It is one of the qualities in them
that I admire most.
As I scoop the beans
with a piece of corn chip

I begin to realize
the importance of fortifying the stomach
before a day of work,
(not sitting around
having intellectual exchanges
but hard labor,
to earn ten tortillas
with meat and rice
and more dark coffee
at the end of the day.)

> *To discern the beauty of a thing*
> *is the finest point*
> *to which we can arrive.*

You hear that sentimental music
playing in the background?

> *I feel as if I had been weeping*
> *over sins that I had never committed,*
> *and mourning over tragedies*
> *that were not my own.*

The morning sun,
white plastic chairs
and the dark-haired senorita
smiling so sweetly at us,

> *Aesthetics make life lovely and wonderful.*
> *...You don't know what it is to fall into the pit,*
> *to be despised, mocked, abandoned, sneered at—*
> *to be an outcast! to find the door shut against one,*
> *to have to creep in by hideous byways,*
> *afraid every moment*
> *lest the mask should be stripped from one's face,*
> *and all the while to hear the laughter,*
> *the horrible laughter of the world,*
> *a thing more tragic than all the tears the world has ever shed.*

We can be here all day
and do the most important thing in the world:
nothing.

Note: lines in italics are quotes from Oscar Wilde.

Philosopher's Way
for George Gonzalez

Thinking has its own laws. It functions of its own accord and does not follow our will. To merge with the object of thought—that is, to direct one's attention to it—is voluntary, but I think perception is the same in this respect: we are able to see what we want to see by freely turning our attention toward it.   —Kitaro Nishida

Arrowheads
carved on limestone blocks
invitation
w
into the physical world
warnings
(the birds sound especially agitated)
memories of George...
cutting stones with workmen in Turkey
feeding us fresh oysters at his house in Bolinas...
a curious elation
blue hills   flowering
follow
George's stones
marking
the
Philosopher's Way.
George…
His eyes are always smiling,
"It's only money."
lovers   trunks entwined   *embracing a tree I cried out:*
she accepts me!
narrow path
generous spirit
crows soar
from sun to shade
lilting a tune
y
the shedding of   a redwood grove
all sound is absorbed into the lush carpet
and one must become reverent

I have my cell phone
in the presence of giants
but don't intend for it to ring.
Fallen   logs
"Hello. Marsha?"
intruder
guardians
of the great divide
which trees, whose limbs?
"Money?…oh!"
"Good morning," a smiling couple.
"I like your pants," she says.
small stone, squarish
asphalt turns into mulch

Have you taken your walk yet?

Have you felt the sun on your body?
Fire and air, the arrowhead shoots up
Is your voice back?
nervous growls   barking dogs   bow-wow-wow
Are you feeling better?
over dry
bridge   creek

Have you napped?
He must think I'm mad. "Cities happen to be problems in organized complexity."
The sky is particularly mauve today, don't you think?
"…No one can tell the whole story."
Do you…?
Pine cones and seeds, needles and buds up ahead a highway, machine noises
on the ground, in the air. The stone points Δ
to the back side of the Bay.

I want to pee, George. Why didn't you design a stone toilet, like the ones we
saw in Ephesus? Really, a man can aim at the bush, but women have to pull down
their pants.

	Shall I be brave	*I dug a hole deep.*
…my bowels began to heave.	or shall I be wild?	*Then I thrust my penis in*
Feeling that I have to bring	Shall I stop and squat	*not without a flash of fear…*
this to the attention of the	and let my gold liquid run free?	
gods, I fetched my palette	Must I be proper	
plate from last night and	or is it not dignified?	
I defecated into the middle of it.	I used to pride myself for holding—	

Buddha sits on the hillside with his shirt off
"Sun's great.
Can't resist."
a philo
Man stands on a park bench
smoking a joint. Loud music blasting
through his earphones.
a glance...
human heads in the bushes.
gang   wars
murders, mayhems,
that was the reputation.
Children playing a rowdy game downhill
blast into the air, "You Stupid!"
"...a then becomes a now."
moss
on stone under shade
the point of departure
is an entrance
entranced, waltz, walk,
though "the erasure of time
already
in
process
even as marks of passage are put down."
Excelsior Ave was

once named

China.

Notes:

"Embracing a tree…" James Broughton, *The Androgyne Journal.*
"Have you taken…don't you think…?" Jack Foley.
"Cities happen to be problems…" Jane Jacobs, *The Life and Death of Great American Cities.*
"…No one can tell the whole story." Barry Lopez, *Artic Dreams,* 1986.
"My bowel began…middle of it." "I dug the hole deep…a flash of fear…" James Broughton,
The Androgyne Journal.
 "…a then becomes a now." Esther Salaman, from *A Collection of Moments.*
"…the erasure of time…" Wendall Berry, *The Art of the Commonplace.*

All quotations except Jack Foley's and James Broughton's can be found in the Philosopher's
Way, McLaren Park, San Francisco.

The vertical line reads:
snowy egret/feathers pearly laced/sugar plum fairy/sun discs/yellow dandelions

A Room In Diyarbakır
November 2011

Turkey—an autumn leaf.

This is the last day of Kurban Bayramı
a religious holiday
commemorating Abraham
sacrificing his only son to God.
Men in suits fill the courtyard.
Women in finery usher in
two young boys
in princely costumes (golden embroidery
on white suits, crowns, capes and scepters).
The sounds of drumming, singing
women ululating—
Between
two fingers
a glow worm
    curls
           "How old are the boys?"
Ma
   smokes
Pa
   smokes
        "Eight and twelve."
High-heeled, manicured sister
with very fine hair
      "She's a jolly chimney."
   smokes.
        "What is the celebration?"
The Imam
   smokes.
One for the cut. Two for the screams.
       "Oh, you know, down there."
The drummer
   smokes.
The singer

smokes.
The procession is slow coming out.
The guests
   smoke.
The waiters
   smoke.
      long semi-translucent tunics over the boys' sparkling white jackets,
but their pants are gone.
     A loud boom in the air.
        A
          shower
    of
        colored
   paper
            petals.
Kurban Bayramı
share what is necessary.
Two-thirds for the poor
one-third to keep.
Cutting of cows and sheep.

Inside a Camii
Kurban Bayramı
the young imam chants.
Men in melodious response
praise Allah, reaffirm faith.

Holiday shopping
a light show in Taksim.
Kurban Bayramı
Plenty of raki
sweet baklavas and honey.

Inside a hotel
five beers two friends and a night mistress
blond hair, red streaks, sturdy as an ox.
Kurban Bayramı
celebrates the flesh.
     I sip

blood-red pomegranate juice
toast to half-bent sister, the crescent moon.

She laughs, her silver teeth tingle my spine
and drench me senseless with the ocean tide.

I lie unclothed on a warm stone,
taste of ambrosia on my tongue.

Her areolas are fruit to my eyes
as she runs her hands over my body and thighs—

*

The Tigris runs shallow,
          A castle ruin atop the hill.
winding idyllically down the canyon.
          At the summit,
Two gigantic stumps, remnants
               weathered tombstones
of an ancient bridge
          dried winter grass.
at a distance upstream.
          A mosque stands at a distance

Mosque and tombstones would witness the disappearance of a village, hundreds of cave dwellings, and the construction of the dam. "Bon bon, bon bon," local urchins run towards the travelers. Their teeth black like old men's.

I taste sheep in my saliva,
coming into the cold
plains of Mesopotamia.
          Thick,
          thick yogurt in a tub.
          Into the bazaar on a donkey's back.
          Vegetables and the morning hubbub.
          Thick, thick yogurt in a tub.
A child sells soap
blackened, dirty soap he salvaged

from the ditches.
At a window
two liras for a cheese pide.
>Flats of eggs and a wailing cub.
>A busy housewife fills her sack.
>Thick, thick yogurt in a tub.
>Into the bazaar on a donkey's back.

The café overlooks
a bejeweled minaret
young men sing around a table
laughter takes over
the guitar strums on.
>Girl runs down the street
>big-eyed girl
>no more than five
>Allah, Allah
>singing her mother's song.
>Mother watches in the shadow
>her black-haired girl in pink
>running down the street
>Allah is charitable.
>Girl of rosebud face
>silver bell voice
>girl holding a little plastic tray
>no more than five
>singing the song Mother taught her
>tiny feet pitter-patter
>pink tunic flapping
>running running Allah Allah
>is charitable.
>One lira. Mother watches.
>One lira. In the shadow.
>Mother watches girl running
>no more than five.
>Plastic slippers, plastic tray
>little rosebud, silver bell
>Have pity, people, have pity.
>The November sun is charitable.

It won't last forever
this, the child, the men, you and me.
The steps of Mardin will survive us all.
Into the lightless alleys, cut-stone walls,
at every bend, the moon.
Your reflection in a night pond
strangely cast,
holding my hand.   ninjas.
                              flying
                    like
                  walls
             the
Cats scale

morning call to prayer
bleating sheep and donkey hooves
outside the window

Evening
deserted

except for a dreary grocery shop
with miserable looking vegetables.
At a street corner
a lone kebab stand has two customers.
The man rolls up bits of grilled meat
in a piece of bread.
The boy takes off down an alley
into a smoke-filled internet café.
Men and boys sitting in small cubicles bark at each other,
drink tea, play video games. A large sign on the wall

red letters and a big **X** over a cigarette.
                    No smoking...something something
                         1000 lira fine,
                    something something...
                         5000 lira fine.

      Daylight is quickly fading at 3:30 in the afternoon. I hurry, trying to catch up with Musefa, a Kurd I met at the courtyard of the Olu Camii.

"We have to be quick," Musefa keeps looking at his watch, "The Dengbejs have been singing since morning. They may not stay at the house for very long."

We tread down one alley after another, cobble-stoned streets and high walls on both sides. Soon I lose sight of his back. A young woman appears beside me.

"Dengbej?" she smiles, walks with me to the next corner and points to her left.

A few old men are leaving as we enter the Dengbej house, but return to a room lined with chairs. One begins to sing. His high tenor voice dwells on a pulsated note, each verse ending with an abrupt sigh. He is Pavarotti in a command performance. In his hand is a string of prayer beads he fingers as he sings. When he is finished he shakes our hands and leaves.

Another man begins. His voice low and husky, his pulsating notes more tremulous. As he sings his eyes gleam and his facial expressions are that of ironic resignation—a story of unrequited love…

A few of the Dengbejs are still in the courtyard when the singing is done. One of them comes up to me.

"Chine?"

"Evet."

He speaks, gesticulating, "…helicopter…".

When he finishes he wants Musefa to translate.

"He said the English word "helicopter" came from the Kurdish language. 'Heli' is bird…"

Their oral tradition has few to pass it on. The Dengbejs will carry their music to their graves, then ride in a helicopter to heaven, where all the angels may gather for a feast of song-story.

Night

Musefa's uncle,

"This is a respectable hotel. No slut."

I close the door.
Residual tremors echo through the building.

Four walls
worn beds
smell of bodies.

The mirror is pride
in the heart of poverty
a cockroach crawls out.
Where am I
is
where I am
there's no toilet paper.
Song-story of love and loss
the old Dengbej sings:
The ocean, the sky, a sheep
I have become
but she doesn't love me.
Pink paint smearing
onto the blue-tiled floor.
The light bulb
naked and bold.
Martyr's images on a TV screen.
Is it such a shock?
The taste of spiced lamb on crisp-baked bread.
The sound of leaking water.
A rippling of dirty white is the window
the plaster an angry slapdash.
The rumbling heater brings some warmth
but comfort is only when I'm fast asleep
dreaming of my father, drowning
(and rescued by my own hands)
instead of imagining the secret police searching
from room to room for PKK sympathizers.
Electricity in mosques and culture centers cut
after sundown.
No call to prayer.
I wait for my escape signal.
It never comes.

*

Murat, god of raki,
you lost my book!
Lord of Sogukçesme,

the glint in your eyes brings me to you.
With dazzling wit
you poke fun at absurdities.
While mortals ponder,
you're gone fishing.

Reappearing at the rooftop kitchen,
chop, dice, grind, shred, stir,
bring down a scrumptious meal to feed a crowd.

Always a crowd.

On a night out you squeeze
seven people into a sedan
and roar into Taksim,
drag a gypsy clarinetist out of his bed.
Then with extended arms
snap fingers,
roll shoulders,
squeal into midnight.

Later, puff smoke like a dragon,
patiently wait for the leaf to return,
to pat you lightly as your mother would
before the first dew
when dreams converse with reality,
the way a tendril
tenderly stretches across the land.

Desolation landscape
dissolves
into glasses of tea.
For every sameness, a sugar cube.
The wind of Marmara flings specks of rain.
Love is a dew drop on the lip.
Night, cold, sits on the bridge.
At the end of the fishing line, a pulse.
"Desire goes out"
despite sleepiness,

"to things as they are in themselves."
A fish, hooked on the roof of its mouth,
writhes.
"Come home," you said.

Note: "Desire goes out to things as they are in themselves." St. Thomas Aquinas.

Tagaq Kronos

spears **Primal mother** stabbing
hunting **earth nectar** knife
knife **hand dance** hunting
(I am a very mature person)
stabbing **erotica** spears
stabbing **shuddering** spears
knife **thighs** hunting
(but nobody knows me.)
hunting **the ground** knife
spears **thunders** stabbing
hehh-haha-hehh
(My friends have a wrong idea of me)
hehh-haha-hehh
hehh-haha-hehh
hehh-haha-hehh
father **pieces of fingers** father
(I am not tame.)
rages **wild flying** rages
drowns **blood ice and water** drowns
his own daughter **birds dogs** his own daughter
(With the talons of an eagle I have weighed tameness.)
his own daughter **calling mother** his own daughter
drowns **mother calling** drowns
rages **calling mother** rages
father **mother calling** father
(O eagle, how sweet is the flight of your wings.)
hehh-haha-hehh
hehh-haha-hehh
hehh-haha-hehh
(Shall you be silent like everything else?)
hehh-haha-hehh
stories **The breath** voices
capillaries **a hawk** susurrus
(Do you perhaps want to write poetry? You shall never write poetry any more.)
susurrus **the tear** capillaries
voices **a fish** stories

voices **gut fire the hands** stories
susurrus **love virulent** capillaries
(Each poem shall be the ripping apart of a poem,)
capillaries **orgasmic love** susurrus
stories **pain pain** voices
(not a poem, but the marks of talons.)
hehh-haha-hehh
hehh-haha-hehh
hehh-haha-hehh
hehh-haha-hehh

Notes:
Tanya Tagaq, Inuit throat singer, performed with the Kronos Quartet in San Francisco, May 11, 2012.
"Decision," poem quoted in parentheses, by Edith Södergran (1892-1923), translated from the Swedish by Jaakko A. Ahokas.

Into the Universe

joyce

stein

keats   basho

duncan

kerouac

mcclure

crane

browning

apollinaire   li po

yeats

plath   cummings

eliot

baudelaire   dickinson

ginsberg   pound

rumi

h a n d h o l d i n g h a n d

Interlude:
the
First
to
/
Poison

The First to Escape

Where there is no beginning or end
there are definitely walls "wars."
The city is divided and conquered.
Subterranean granite and marble
all cages are rectangular.

Enter. Exit.

Pigeons barred by nets
their feet pricked from wire stubs
lay down on the ledges.

Cubicles are not for flying objects.

Animals and humans had a common language
once, back in the Ice Age.

In the white pyramid, eighteen elevators go
up forty-eight levels of internment, one
more gritty than the other.

The subdivision—room within room
within room
until you find yourself sitting in the toilet
of a single stall.

"You're an individual, you have a choice,"
the ads say.
But the man sleeping on the street?

Rag doll on sidewalk,
long curls hide the shame.
Tattered covering, squalid feet,
whiskey mixed with piss.
Stubble mug, vacant stare,
obscure tongue muttering

at pedestrians, at dogs,
at himself on shit-filled sheet.

Rag doll on sidewalk,
crouching in a heap
Once a bundle wrapped in cloth,
now ravaged by a grave disease.
Those strong arms carting you
are not your savior's.
It's their job to come once a week
here to clean the street.

and the munchkin with a long pole balancing
two plastic bags of aluminum cans
on his shoulders
and the two Chinese women sitting
next to each other on the bus,
breasts folding on top of stomachs
on top of thighs.
chitchatting in Cantonese
eating kumquats, spitting out the little seeds,
listening to the graffiti warning
spoken in English, Spanish, and Chinese
watching the bus filling up with Latinos, blacks,
whites and Asians,
passing McDonald's and Walgreens
Safeway and Bank of America

while their children lay down their money at the altar
and recite the litany:
Quarter Pounder, Diet Coke, apple pie, milk shake.

Communion is with the guts.
Absolution is temporal fulfillment.
Faith is knowing they can return anytime
to the same place with the same sign and the same smell.

White,
blanketing the mountain range.

Blast, blast the mines.
Tell secrets
 Obama to Sarkozy on Netanyahu,
near
a waterfall,
 "I have to deal with him every day."
Her virginal gown
 Oh chain can you see?
his circumcision suit
 Or is it power-play?
to be entered to be cut.
Things we don't know
or don't want to know—
 doves in a gilded cage.
Bleached skin dyed hair
fair is fair.
   "If white isn't an ethnic group, what is it?"
   "I think it's *an assertion of power.*"
  "*Take up the white man's burden,*"
said the young Asian man, "*but stop taking my women.*"
And that light which guides us into eternity,
that calming, all encompassing mercy,
is, as the story goes…
  "Life, like a dome of many-coloured glass
   Stains the white radiance of Eternity."

 Sin is OK, as long as you say "I'm sorry."
A French maid's apron prettily starched.
 for monsieur
C major on the piano keys.
 The great highway has no stop sign.
The walls, bedspreads,
 satin sheets
lamp shades
 crystal meth
in pallid sheen;
elegant, fastidious, classy—
  clean? I ONCE BUILT A SNOWMAN
    AND PUT HIM IN THE HALL

WITH A WHITE MAN
THERE'S NO MAN
    AT...
The graves
after all the miseries done to this world
we decay under white stones.

My eyes open to yours
washed gentle and somnolent after love.

They have become delusive
in the ordinariness of things
haunting

tinting the thought, they dwell
in the recesses of speech.
Those eyes

a token...

You play music
fingers circling
the rim of a petal.
With each round
the ripples tighten
into a whole note
held
tremulous

The distance between notes
is breath.
Intake
a swell of acceptance
outtake
a mark of surrender

Where the notes linger

in your hands
you play music
coaxing a whisper
into an arching passage

Elsewhere
drips
the nectar
of a flower

in adagio.

Headline: Key Hmong Denied Arlington Burial
Feb 4, 2011

Vang Pao,
it is better that you remain in Fresno
where your people love you,
where the streets are filled with the aroma of grilled sausages and rice,
where young girls wear platform shoes,
and young men tie checkered cotton sashes over their peasant pants,
where women in cross-ribbed headdresses and kimono-like skirts dance,
and men gong in the afternoons
to drive out bad spirits.

It is better that you remain in Fresno
where your people may visit you often
and bring flowers and wine,
where they may call out your name,
and you may hear them loud and clear
and soothe their sorrow in their dreams.
You have fought a lot of wars
but the battles are still raging.
Isolation of the old
fury of the young
living in a land that ignores their privation.

It is better that you remain in Fresno.

The little headstones in Arlington will
white-wash you.
Some may think heroes
should all be buried together;
but a hero belongs
to the people who find him meaningful
in the scorching heat
in the biting cold
in the dusty flatland
in California Central Valley.

Water in the sink, dark drops splashing
the counter, wetting wall, floor, body,
hair—long, silken hair of the cloudy
"soup"—and the Indian cotton skirt
scrubbed, twisted, squeezed. Whirled
in the water, color loosens with the hair.
Skinny dipping lucent strands drift
in octopus ink: living and non-living things
are mostly inseparable.

The water isn't black, though the skirt and hair
look black: black is dark things, dark things black.
Berries make dye; charcoal was once eyeliner.
Composite seaweed stirring in cold water washing.
The suggestion never crosses the mind as black but
indigo, the crushed berry skin tart on the tongue.

Running
down the hall
fire-escape window bobbing
up and down in the frame.
She giggles.
He laughs,
"Door door door door!"
Someone opens a door.
She swings

catches the big man's chin.
Oh so thick with little black hair.
Haha, don't stop.
Something squeaks. Look down.
A plate of leftover rice and stale vegetables,
chopsticks, tea cup, what else?
OK. Keep moving
left
right
stay away everybody!
Where's Bryan?
Room 306.
Let's go.
Run faster.
Knock knock, Bryan.
Nothing. Just saying hi.
BYE! Go on, go
into the elevator,
brother,
catch that door!

*

Last destination
(meticulously mapped out)
blurred by rain water.

Waltz under a red bridge named Golden
the sun is always setting.
She smiles as she makes a sandwich,
"I'm just glad to have a job."
So is her boss. Just glad. Glad. Just
to be inside where there's a bed
and a refrigerator. No one argues
with them about that.

Police don't know what has been committed
in a quiet room…

Fitting spherical, heavenly bodies
into a catacomb
In the labyrinth, who is the sentinel?
When we run away we get caught
and fall down and promise
not to stray again
but be good citizens
walking the grid knowing all the time
there are much more than sentences
subjects and subjugation

that the breath is the first to escape

there

my flying object!

Notes:
"If white isn't an ethnic group..." Jack Foley, "Multiculturalism and the Media."
"Take up..." Rudyard Kipling, "The White Man's Burden."
"Life, like a dome..." Percy Bysshe Shelley, "Adonais."
"I ONCE BUILT..." Jack Foley, "Multiculturalism and the Media."

Poison

A reason to live
blooming Blood Blossom
paces the room
puffs cigarettes
crackling on the keyboard
vermin in rosewater
heat, hate
eat, ate
gnaw their way
into the typos
Love is
Dead.

Duncan was skinny and tall with long greasy hair parted in the middle. His face had an angry outburst of pimples, making it impossible for him to shave between the swellings. The girls said he was weird. I didn't know what they meant.

Like most middle school personalities, Duncan had a sidekick: Crystal, eighth grade, tiny like a mouse beside a flagpole. They went everywhere together. When big Mavis moved into the dormitory, she started hanging out with them too.

The trio, odd as they were, never excluded anyone who showed an interest in being their friend. It was toward the end of the school year when I felt comfortable enough to be in their company that I understood what others meant by "weird."

They were talking about someone that Duncan didn't like.

"We finally put him to sleep," Duncan said as a matter of fact.

I didn't understand "put him to sleep."

"It means he killed him," Mavis explained.

"How?"

"Voodoo," Duncan looked at me darkly, "Me and my friends put a curse on him."

Crystal with his big wide eyes nodded vigorously,

"Yeah, he really did."

long-life   noodles
                sweet   and   sour   pork
        salt   or   was it
                         MSG
            empty   into   the   gutter
press   on the   eyes   warm hands
        keep   them   from   bulging
                                    meditate
on   the wings   of   a   butterfly
                        its stillness   in time
                            of   peace
        the   havoc
                            when   it   quakes

"Every dish has a bit of MSG, my friend," said the wise man, "Drink Coca-Cola.
Fight poison with poison. Two negatives will bring a positive change."

∴

My face
        I'm a little red cupcake
is the face
        with sour cream on top.
you wished for
        I enjoy being eaten
preserved by the science of man
        I like being red because
a beautiful face
        red denotes passion and delight
you can stare at
        and though I'm topped by sour cream
a while longer
        the cream has been sweetened,
than at grandma and grandpa's
        my sour cream...
faces.

"When anecdotal evidence pointed to a slowing in the rate of decay among human bodies from the 1960s to 1980s, some attributed this to the presence of preservatives from processed food. Nutrition and food author Seth Roberts speculated in 2009 that these preservatives may not directly impact the rate of decay, but perhaps act to diminish the presence of some bacteria that play a role in the decomposition process." *Whoa I have so many preservatives in me, I'll live forever!*

∴

Sssssssssssssss

sip

secrete

sweet   sensory   Dior   song

seduction   secret   satin   scintillate

sanguine

sin

Spray

into air

step

into vapors

do

not

ingest

I squeezed two drops into
my step-mother's open mouth
watched them disappear
on her tongue
She slept
no longer able to put up a fight
I went back to the kitchen to make lunch

∴

Notes:
"The Effect of Food Preservatives on the Human Body"---Rob Callahan, May 28, 2011.
"I'm a little red cupcake"---Jack Foley.
"Spray into air..." instructions on how to put on the perfume "Poison" by Christian Dior.

Like
Water:
Tao-te
Ching
&
Complications

Tao
to speak it
is not the extraordinary Tao.
Name
to name it
is not the extraordinary name.
Absence is the beginning
of heaven and earth.
Presence is the mother
of ten-thousand things.
Therefore be absent
so as to behold the wonder of Tao,
be present
so as to behold the limitation of things.
These two
emerge together with different names
and together they are mysterious.
Mystery upon mystery—
the door to all wonders.   is it

                                    heaviness
                                    lightness

                                  already it is

                              euphoric the mouth
                              euphoric the nipples
                              euphoric the penis
                                    liquid
                                      e
                                      x
                                      c
                                      h
                                      a
                                      n
                                      g
                                      e

Ahhhhhhhhhhhh
AHHHHHHHHHH
AHHHHHHHHHH
HUNGER

All under heaven know what beauty is.
That is, ugliness.
All know what good is:
evil.
Absence and presence are born together.
Hardship and ease complete each other.
Long and short are shaped together.
High and low lean on each other.
Music and sound harmonize together.
Front and back follow each other.
Therefore the sage does things that are absent,   from nothing
teaches without speaking,
does not judge the workings of ten-thousand things
produces but does not own,   still
services without pride,
does not rest in accomplishment.   stoic
The one who does not rest in accomplishment   .
shall never cease.   trickle of sound
                                                                                         distill
                                                                                         distill
                                                                                             .

                                                                                   from one thread
                                                                                         link
                                                                                       extract
                                                                                             .

                                 MOVE
                                                                                      extend
                                                                                      retract
                                                                                             .

                                                                                             .

By not esteeming the worthy   store
the mass will not engage in rivalry.
By not valuing goods that are difficult to come by
the mass will not steal.

By not displaying the desirables
the mass's heart will not be confused.
Therefore this is how the sage rules:
humble the heart
fortify the stomach
weaken ambition
strengthen the bone.
Let the mass be absent from shrewdness and desire
so that even the clever ones won't dare to act.
Act without acting
and all is cured.

Many Eyes sees many things.
Many things does Many Eyes see.
It sees.
It likes.
It wants.
It keeps.
Many Eyes keeps many things.
Many Eyes has a headache
for having so many things.
It doesn't know where to put this.
It doesn't know where to put that.
It doesn't know where.
It doesn't know.
Many Eyes has a headache.
It doesn't want.
Many Eyes closes one eye.
Many Eyes closes two.
Many Eyes keeps closing its eyes
until only one is open.
Its headache is gone.
Many Eyes keeps only one eye
open.

The Tao rushes
and yet to use it, it never overflows.
An abyss,
like the ancestor of ten-thousand things,
blunts what is sharp,

untangles what is quarrelsome,
blends what is bright,
companion to what is dust.
Oh deep as death but it exists.
I don't know whose offspring it is—
before the appearance of the Yellow Emperor.

The time when the head flew out of the body
not caring about severed ties
or plunging into icy water
or bouncing out of the sphere
The time when no one was able to catch it
or even got a glimpse of its properties
Everyone dismissed it as a flying saucer.
Everyone had a head on the body.
Everyone, except one
body without a head
doing doing doing

Heaven and Earth are merciless.
They let all things live and die.
The sages are merciless.
They treat the mass like straw dogs.
The space between heaven and Earth,
isn't it like a bellows?
Empty but does not collapse,
use it, and more comes out.
Excessive words debilitate.
Better to guard the center.

What? It's time to get up?
Time to get dressed
have breakfast, brush teeth?
it's time to go?
What?
You can't wait? I'm dragging my feet?
I'm too slow, I have no drive?
What?
You don't like my attitude?

I'm pretending just to aggravate you?
I'm making you mad?
Eh, what did you say to me last night?
Did I do my homework?
Did I? Did I?
It's too late now?
Too late?
What?
You're leaving now?
What do I do then?
You don't care?

The Valley Spirit does not die.
It is called the mysterious female.
The opening of the mysterious female
is the root of heaven and earth.
Softly, gently, it exists.
Use it without effort.

                        First rose, long stem
                          romance of your lips
                            testing, tasting,
                          pink turns crimson
                            stem shivers
                           petals scatter
                      one between my eyes
                       two on my breasts
                          and the rest
                         like all others
                  slip casually to the floor.

Heaven is eternal. Earth is everlasting.
They last forever
because they are not nurtured in order to survive.
Therefore they are everlasting.
The sage puts his body in the back
and becomes the one in front.
Puts his body on the outside
and is able to preserve it.
Isn't it because of his selflessness
that he may realize the self?

At a bustling street corner
an old nun
touches the face
of a young soldier, asks,
"What is your wish?"

He replies, "I want to make love."

Highest good is like water.
Water benefits all things
but does not compete.
It lies in the lowest place
which all men disdain.
Therefore it is close to the Tao.
Dwell in goodness
with a heart good and deep.
Do good to others.
Speak in good faith.
Govern with good system.
Perform with good capability.
Act in good time.
If only man does not compete
there will be no strife.

               e kil is like illi
               ek illi illi ke ke

       e eats, like egret one foot illi illi the water flows
               ek, it calls   ek ek
               no ill   like all is perfect

                        the cloud
    the sky   the water
                        the air
               as if all ills are killed   illiilli

                        as if   is like
         like   ekil   kile
               is "tickle" in Norwegian

a figure being tickled Kekekeke

illi illi the egret wades illi illi

as if ekil is like

Holding onto something that is overflowing—
it is better to stop.
Fitting a short beam on the roof—
it won't last for long.
A hall filled with gold and jade
cannot be guarded.
Riches and honors breed arrogance
causing one's own downfall.
Withdraw when work is done—
the way of heaven.

knife cannot cut
water
water cannot separate
land
land cannot divide
man

blink

and all is not well again

Body and soul embrace.
   Can they not be separated?
The vital breath is soft.
   Can it be like that of an infant?
The Mysterious Vision is cleansed.
   Can it be without blemish?
Love the country, govern the people.
   Can it be done without strategy?
The gate of heaven opens
   Can it be without the Female?
Having enlightenment in four directions
   Can it be from ignorance?

Grow and domesticate,
propagate without claim,
service without pride,
lead without supremacy.
This is called the Mysterious Virtue.

Note: This selection cosists of Chapters 1-10 of Lao Tzu's *Tao-te Ching*.

We
Shall
Be
Changed

Lunch Talk

Under
the dome of God
a black sheep

Baa the white sheep gather sheepishly wondering how to approach with a question
that won't hurt anyone's feelings or shake the foundation of friendship but will ulti-
mately triumph by washing the sin off the sinner's back turning black back to white
they bow their heads and pray O God O.

black sheep
suggests
"Someone's already asked why I don't go to church."

Baa the white sheep sigh discreetly and are much encouraged by the courageous
brother who has taken such a step in making it much easier for them to show their
concern over the salvation of their friend and one of them asks cheerfully, "So what
did you say to that question?"

"I have no need for church,"
black sheep
laughs

Baa the white sheep laugh too and go back to eating it is better to have a good time
eating and talking about old times and all the silliness they did when they were
young than to engage in what might spoil the appetite after all they've made an effort
and that's probably good enough.

under
the dome of God
three sheep
baaaaa

The Monkey King Makes an Offering

To appease my late mother and stepmother with a pagan ceremony of food and clothing, I, the Monkey King (Big Saint of Heaven's Equal, Trickster) borrow the wrong fan from the Iron Fan Princess and nearly singe my tail...much like the time when I somersaulted to the end of the world, only to be trapped in the Goddess of Mercy's palm.

I make this offering on behalf of my father, who is straddling between two worlds.

wind fans fanning dry heat parched throat
earth god pounds his pestle on the hollowed midriff
incense rising fan fanning a slither of titter inviting all shadows
to break seven years of drought and famine
desirous one you shall not perish by the hands of your dead wives
vying for supremacy on the bank of amber spring
new clothes thin as paper mimosa flutter up
dark specks of blind spots orange in their scent
moving toward away the operatic bravado of a single
note
count the silence the blooming red
petal by petal five columns on the edge of the world
marred by graffiti and piss
the fire leaps seven bounds with each fanning
incinerating the flesh   an offering
pain pierces in the direction of nascency
big saint of heaven's equal trickster in a command performance
bearing fatty pork a whole chicken and three cups of wine
crossing over to the other side
what remains   a turn of mercy's hand

Notes:

"The Monkey King"—a character from the Chinese classic, *Journey to the West.*

"amber spring"—underworld.

"five columns on the edge of the world"—The Monkey King mistook the Goddess of Mercy's five fingers for the columns at the end of the world. In order to prove to the Goddess that he had been there, he carved his name on one of the "columns" and peed. The Goddess opened her hand and showed him that he had done nothing but pee and write on her fingers: he had in fact been nowhere.

"a turn of mercy's hand"— determines the fate of the devotee.

backwash

i keep thinking you're unhappy
>*The end of the world has no story*

you keep thinking i'm unhappy
>*Like Christmas with angels and glory*

he keeps thinking i will make him happy
>*A kid says, "No way!"*

she keeps thinking i am in the way....
>*No fun and no play*

i keep thinking you are thinking
>*No gifts, no blood-letting gory?"*

that maybe she is thinking incorrectly
>*No gifts, no blood-letting gory*

she keeps thinking that maybe you are thinking
>*No fun and no play*

that everything is okay.
>*A kid says, "No way!"*

mother, father, lover, brother, sister
>*Like Christmas with angels and glory*

choose your weapon
>*The end of the world has no story*

—Deborah Wenzel/*Clara Hsu*

Nit in a Faux Mink

advanced ingenuous life imitates form imitates life ingenuous advanced
womb existence not an accident not an accident this manufactured stroke-able
fiber of solace solace for the soulless the soulless parasite of fiber of solace
egg into legs into needles stitching into egg into legs into needles stitching into
life leaps on dead skin on dead skin leaps life
Keep up the God work O dear God the work
life leaps on dead skin on dead skin leaps life
egg into legs into needles stitching into egg into legs into needles stitching into
fiber of solace solace for the soulless the soulless parasite of fiber of solace
womb existence not an accident not an accident this manufactured stroke-able
advanced ingenuous life imitates form imitates life ingenuous advanced

SIN

"I live in terror of not being misunderstood." Oscar Wilde.

Sin is an essential element of progress.
Without it the world would stagnate
or grow old,
or become colorless.

In its rejection of the current notions
about morality
it is one with the higher ethics.

Nature
cares little
about chastity.

The mere existence of conscience,

the faculty of which
people prate so much nowadays,
and are so ignorantly proud,
is a sign
of our imperfect development.

Indeed, I fear that
the inartistic temperaments of the day
busied themselves also
in the matter of literature and art,
for the accusations
of plagiarism were endless,
and such accusations
proceed either from
the thin colorless lips of impotence,
or from the grotesque mouths of those
who possessing nothing of their own,
fancy that they can gain a reputation for wealth
by crying out that they have been robbed.

You, my children,
You're not good enough.
You don't finish school,
don't visit, don't write,
never even send me a card
on my birthday.
Only when YOU need SOMETHING
do I hear from you.
You live with your boyfriend/girlfriend
won't get married, don't want children
spend your money on dogs and cats.
My friends said don't even think
they'll take care of you in your old age.
Well, I don't!
And neither do I want to be grandma.
You've been trouble
since the day you were born.

Look at me. Look at me!
I used to have a figure.
Then I cooked
I cleaned
I slaved away
I sacrificed
Now I look like a bucket.
What for? What for?
You took my beauty.
You took my youth.
You took my life.
I get nothing in return.
Nothing!
See?
I have been robbed!

All art is immoral.

> *They say it's a sign of the time*
Bad artists always admire each other`s work.
> *most young people just can't care less*
They call it being large-minded
> *but dream and dream all night and day.*
and free of prejudice.
> *It's because life is too easy*
But a truly great artist
> *so they drive their parents crazy.*
cannot conceive of life being shown,
> *Dream and dream those big heads away.*
or beauty fashioned,
> *Play is more important than work*
under any conditions
> *and that`s the long and short of it.*
other than those he has selected.
> *Go ahead. Keep it up. Bon voyage.*
> > *love, mom.*

Art is out of reach of morals,
for her eyes are fixed upon things beautiful
and immoral
and ever-changing.

Note:
Excerpts (in regular font) from Oscar Wilde, *The Critic As Artist.*

Like Cereal
Like Ceres

So much stuff within the confinement
To: The Girl
limitless for the imagination
Between this breath
one cockcrow another inferno
and the next
a net that spreads wide catching
a moth escapes through
a worm here a bell there
your lips
the heart, oh the heart is weak
It flutters toward the evening light
under the hypnotic drone.
gets caught on the gauze curtain
On and on it races against the train

the whistle! A warning a wakeup call
Death means do not disturb
a vision an invitation to a dance
The next breeze
trees with their roots facing the sky
sends the moth into the garden
long-feathered leaves piercing
I glimpse a shape dancing
a crown down earth down to home
feathers plumage rising from its bone mask
down into an alcove of cracked nerves.

Is it true after all we are water
Is it you?
just plain old water not wine not juice
Is it you?
and when we are sucked dry we
Is it you?

become clay / broken little pieces of grey stuff when scattered
  The fog is writhing down the hill
onto the forest floor they whiten
  In a moment all turns milky white
the surface like snow.

My Son Likes to Get Lost in the City

My son likes to get lost in the city.
He says,
"Nothing's more thrilling than walking
uphill when you remember going down
or turning at a particular corner
where there's supposed to be a
bright green Victorian house
only to run into a Safeway parking lot."

"I know my directions."
And he does.
If he finds the ocean in front of him
it's time to turn back.
It's not hard to get back to the center of town.

My son likes to take the bus when he's tired of walking.
And if he does end up in some boring neighborhoods
all he has to do is to cross the street
and hop on the opposite bus.

My son doesn't like to read street signs.
He recognizes landmarks
like this great big poster of Spider-man on a wall
or this really tall building that looks like a castle
or this steep hill that is especially hard to climb
or this gnarly tree that looks like a dragon in flight.
He says he knows his way better
when he visualizes the city
instead of memorizing street names.
They have no meaning to him.

My son likes to get lost in the city
and I never know where he has been.
He always manages to come back
hungry and tired,
his long arms dangling beside his skinny legs,

his full lips muttering about
some new discoveries
and his eyes bright from fresh air and exercise.
My son won't walk the city any other way.
It is a city of his own making
a chaotic, fantastical Chutes and Ladders
rolling from hill to hill
dipping into fog
burning in the sun.

The Juliad

Of august gold-wreathed
and beautiful Aphrodite I shall sing...

August night

the womb sheds
a replica.

She grew
already grown
sat ornery
on a Chinese chest
kicking the elaborately carved surface
of languid women in an ancient garden.

long arms
thin leg
she could not say the alphabet.
Big tears
tight fists
she only knew one plus one equals---
the sum of yum.
Sweet chrysanthemum
spun
in a white dress
when she felt the blues,
was well known for group fights in school.
Wrestled boys, pinned them down
never refused a challenge.
Wrote rivers of words
behind closed doors
only her pet rat could read them.

In time she learned to please
did laundry, dishes
when she needed money to spree.
With wobbly footing

in Yin and Yang
she declared, "I want the part."
Pumped abdomen two hundred times a day.
Clipped eyebrows into neat twin crescents.
Painted red fingernails and purple toenails.
Went to all her classes.
Smiled brilliantly, continuously,
NOTICE ME! With every ounce
of energy she twirled and whirled
and stretched and leaped,
"I want to be prima ballerina."

They smiled back.
Lovely girl, worked so hard.
Such expressions and confidence,
she could really do the part.
The buzz was on, meekly at first,
"I'm it, I'm it…"
then like a breeze it swelled
from dressing room into the hall, booming,
"She's it, she's it!"
Ever heard teenage girls scream?
Hugs and kisses followed
by tears, a drop or two.
"Mom!" she turned,
eyes bursting with light,
suddenly
Clara.

> *Who was more beautiful? / Who was the one without a love?*
> *lines appeared where there were none before*
> *snow flakes*
> *shimmering down the darkened stage*

Let
the wrinkles on my face gather you
Get in the car!
the warmth of my palm relieve the throb
Step on the gas!
Let my tears melt the broken glass

The tires screech
you haphazardly glue
    I'm not coming back.
my breath to slow the tempest
    Head south.
that dims your smile.
    Turn up the radio.
When you were very young
    Fill the head with noise.
you climbed onto my lap
    Incessant, pathetic noise
with your chubby feet
    that sustains the pulse.
held my downcast head
    The truck ahead is too slow.
dotted kisses on my cheeks.
    Curse it. Change lane. Speed up.
Your wispy hair
    Trees are running backward.
brushed my face
    Lamp posts turn into silver streamers.
and in that moment
    299 miles to Los Angeles.
I saw crimson azaleas
    Rest stop? No rest.
that bloomed in the window box.
    When you stop you have to think.
    The ghosts you left behind:
    mother's sad eyes
    father's fury
    the bitchy friends you love.
    It is night.
    The man beside you smokes a cigarette.
    You are his now.
    He is yours.

    Fern of the forest—

An old man read a love poem in front of the Trieste in North Beach:

> *Clara, High, Apart*
> *Throw your wings out to the stars, to the storm, to the sea;*
> *Take what makes itself a tomorrow for your flight.—*

You held your red kickboxing gloves high and belched like a man.

    Jube ·
        Jewel ·
               Jules ·
                       Julia ·

Amity is sipping tea
on the sidewalk of Istanbul
sharing a fish sandwich
by the Sea of Marmara.
Sleeping in a cave
lulled by soft dust that
fell on our clothes
our bodies scrubbed clean
under the ancient dome.

◆

    Little Face,
Today I passed by The Zephyr Cafe
and looked in through the window.
Of course, you weren't there.
But for me,
looking had become a habit
and I saw no reason to break it.
One time you waved me into the cafe
when you recognized my long yellow turban.
Do the people you see in Portland
have such signature attire?
I walked down to the gargantuan apartment building
where you and Brent had lived
and thought of the time you dropped
your keys down the laundry chute.

I chuckled
imagining your shocked expression.
This was another grey day in San Francisco
but the wind had died down.
The walk to Safeway was quite pleasant.
But you must have grumbled when you went to buy groceries
in the winter, in the rain and bitter cold.
What is it like for you now,
to be away?
What kind of loneliness permeates your days
and what kind of liberation do you feel
in this loneliness?
Earlier this evening when I was at my desk,
Cookie slept on my pillows between my back
and the back of the chair.
I had forgotten that she was there.
When I got up she went plop
onto the seat.
I picked her up. Cookie, Cookie, I stroked her.
She wasn't hurt but smelled of sleep
like the scent of a baby girl…
Another memory surfaces as I write this,
of cradling you in my arms.
And another, of holding your hand.
Since you left, memories are what I hang onto.
They are all beautiful
even when there was sadness.

◆

She emerged
from the waves of the resounding sea
restored her body on a fallen log.
          Anantasana, the sleeping Vishnu
          wakened.
She lifted her wings
                              a squeal of delight
firefly
rising

Notes:

"Of august gold-wreathed...I shall sing" and "She emerged from the waves of the resounding sea," *Homeric Hymn 6 to Aphrodite.* Translated by Apostolos Athanassakis.

"Clara, High, Apart" beginning lines of a poem by Peter Sherburn-Zimmer.

Anantasana (sleeeping Vishnu) and firefly are yoga poses.

We Shall Be Changed

"Did they change your life?" Jack Foley asked me, commenting on someone's poetry. I never thought of poems being life-changing. At least it is not what I think about when I attend a reading or pick up a collection of poetry. "Life-changing" is a tall order. Do poets set out to change lives when they write? If not to change others, does the poet's writing change the poet? If a poem is to have a place in the universe, what part of the alchemy does it play?

There are poems that I remember. I remember them because they are meaningful to me. They are meaningful because they touch a part of me that was not touched before. If I get a glimpse of something unknown, I have already changed.

"...but we shall all be changed, in a moment, in the twinkling of an eye." (*1 Corinthians* 15:52)

EXCELSIOR

He was a teenager the first time he touched a piano. The tones of the instrument vibrated through his entire body. He was instantly obsessed, ran to Morrison Street's flea market and bought as many sheet music pieces as he could afford, brought them home and started to decipher the scores. He would listen to his brother and his friend play music on the violin and piano. He would listen to the radio and the recordings of Beethoven's "Moonlight Sonata" until every note was committed to memory. He would play the piano in the church when it was not in use, play until the "Moonlight Sonata" flowed from his fingers without effort.

1956

He hasn't slept all night.
something persistent
is circling in his mind—
Mendelssohn's *Song Without Words*.
Its melody, a prayer,
fervent yet restrained.
The broken chords
on the left hand
roll like a murmuring brook.
This song,
Now excited
　　　now worrying
　　　　　now impatient.
The man lets his fingers
idle down a few keys
but he dares not play.
He pulls out a thin, white towel
from his grey pants
and wipes his face and neck.
He takes a deep breath,

1967

This is a factory
of fluffy gold
sawdust pyramids,
Hammers and copper,
wires and felt.
Men pushing a piano
into the crate
sweaty shoulders
cursing the one final shove
before lunch.

Noise!
This is a factory
not a conservatory.
　　　Noise!
music is not made here
　　　not in a factory.
Only pianos.
　　　Only pianos.

Ping.

2012

A tinge of nasty buzz
in the voice today.
There might be a piece of
fuzz accidentally
got stuck between the keys.
Or the pebbles
in the glass vase sitting
on top of the case
decide to rattle
in protest of the plastic
yellow and red blossoms,
so alive
yet so dead, (no need of water)
in the likeness of mums.
　　　Fake
　　　is never the sound
　　　that comes out of this piano.
Every movement is an emotion.

Little fisted hands,

sucking in the moist and
suffocating air.

A faint smell of saw dust
wafts into the room.
Where he is sitting
there are ten upright pianos
Each has a bronze color-plated name:
E X C E L S I O R

Ring ring…ring ring…the telephone!
"Yes. Yes," he jumps to his feet.
"It's a girl!"
The melody flows
like a young leaf sailing
down a steady stream.
He plays it now, on the piano.
His heart
his heart
is rippling with music.

Strike a note
ping ping ping ping
The elusive pitch squiggles
between each turn
of the tuning lever.
(Try catching a frog
with a pair of soapy hands.)
The wood is seasoned
on the rooftop.
         This is a factory

ever upward
not a conservatory
no music
is played here.
            noise!
            noise!
sweat and curse.
Gloria
in Excelsis
Deo.

         too young to know
to touch to caress to make music.
Standing on the precipice
of adulthood
the knowledge of love
is yet to be revealed.
Only ignorance
marches up and down,
"If it ain't white, it's black."

Who will play you?
Who will play you like rain drops
on the surface of water? The ripples
that swell first, then disappear
carry a substance
too hard to describe.
Concepts, not actions.
The body feels
      in mysterious ways.
Feel the body.

Hong Kong, 1948

by reading books.

The first European slim line was produced.

He learned to build a piano

for my father, James Ma.

Mad House Fantasia and Fugue

Fantasia—

Knowledge knows no ledge
now
the wizard cannot tell night from day.
He asks his apprentice, "What should I do?"
His wand, tiny like the sprout
of a lily's bulb
liquid gold freely discharging.
They try to catch each drop
with a tubular vessel without much success.
"It's all your fault," cries the wizard. His names are many.

The angel comes
in the form of a farmer; bad teeth, slim and muscular. He has endured turbulent
times. Knowing the wizard's trouble, the angel says, "Nay n'ho yum gum dor s-hui."
And the wizard scowls, "I don't know what you're talking about. You don't speak
my language. Be gone!" But the angel folds his wings over the wizard's ears and
patiently repeats the words, knowing that he is deaf.

O my daughter,
you travel from the underside
of the earth
to be near me.
I call to you, "Hello, hello."
And you pat my back and say, "Accept your fate."
I'm embarrassed. I'm fearful.
I want to tell you things but I can't.
I'm confused by my own magick.

She drifts in and out of the wizard's sight
bringing him baskets of fruits and sweets.
(She has just made love inside a secret cavern, with wild things howling at the
entrance. Her lover hummed an ancient tune, ethereal, haunting…)
She is his daughter and lover. She is his mother.
He crouches on the throne while she trims his claws.
She shaves his head. There is no need for furnishing.

Two minutes is not sufficient. It must be three.
Five is too much, and all will be burned.
"Move!" commands the wizard, "the lights are going out."
The elixir of sleep is stirred and drunk.
The clock is meaningless as no one keeps time.

fugue—

Turn on the light.
It's dark here.
I'm sick and
you don't even know it.
Don't even know
   day and night have lost their cloaks. Naked they are, sexless.
   It's three in the morning. It's dark here. Go back to sleep.
     White mice circling around the ceiling lamp. Turn on the light.
               Turn on the light.
  dark here,
   dark here,
there is no turning (telling) which one is which. My daughter, I'm sick. What
should I do?
   Lie down, back to bed. It's what you must do. Lie down. In darkness,
   the light—
It's early. It's late. I'm hungry. I'm not.
      I'm not hungry, I am
  many things are yet to be done and you don't even know
Rock-a-bye baby on the treetop. When the wind blows…you don't even know.
        馬生, 早晨. 你好嗎? People coming
and going. Faces. Noise. Night. Day. Darkness. Light. Turn on the light and you'll
know and you'll see that I'm sick.
你唔好自己起身行呀. 等我嚟幫你. 唔係一陣又跌倒. King Lear, the heath is
full of ghosts.
  cello and piano
   entwines
   bemoans
  a young man's laughter rings fearless in the open space.
Soon

they too will disappear. It's dark here and you don't even know it.

Hey, hey, wake up.   Wake up.

老人家要多飲的湯水.   馬生   飲多的湯水. So much to do. So little time. Are you sure everything is secured? I'm not sure I'm sick. I'm in the dark,

don't even know

He told me to stay back. Said no,   no,   no, and then he fell.

The furniture! Move it from one room to another. Preserve it! Calligraphy all over the floor, walls, ceilings. Turn on the light!

She is writing me a message. There. She's impatient. Can't you see it's dark here? Look how she shakes the mailbox.

Turn on the light.

You don't see. Don't know

My father was born on Twelfth Night.

He woke at three in the morning.

My father loved music.

He couldn't go back to sleep.

My father learned to build a piano.

He was groggy and nervous.

My father opened a factory in Hong Kong.

He waited for his friends to arrive.

My father sold his pianos all over the world.

He smiled when his old quartet showed up.

My father immigrated to America.

He drank chickpea soup and ate barbecue chicken.

My father built a world music shop in San Francisco.

He sang Happy Birthday with them.

My father suffered a stroke while playing the cello.

He blew out all the candles.

My father had to retire.

He ate his chocolate cake.

My father turned ninety on Twelfth Night.

He clapped his hands and said thank you.

馬生 *Don't know it. Don't see.* 等我嚟幫你

Who are you? Don't remember. ..Who am I? HA! You don't even know it.   I'm just kidding.

Did he sleep?   Did he pee?   Did he eat?

He is sick and he doesn't even know it.

The big washer woman took up half the bathroom. She scared him.

Here, I'm sick, and my forehead is marked with ash.

瞓得唔夠兩個字又起床. 行出行入, 無停過.
        How long?   How frequent?   How much?
乜都比佢食清   Am I ?   唔係嘛
      Hello. Hello. There!   Hello? Hello there.
No one will bother if he is put in a home.
      I touch my father's hair
      long, full, white below the crown.
           He sits still
           wrapped in a bed sheet.
      I snip, easy, quick,
      thin the thickness with a rough cut.
           The bristles fall,
           pepper his shoulders.
      My cold steel presses
      nearer and nearer his scalp.
           He is at my mercy.
      Holding small patches of hair at a time
      I trim them between my fingers
           and bend his ears, blade touching skin
           going from behind, around and up.
      His eyes are fixated on the soundless TV.
           Using a comb, I even the stubble.
           My palm curves over the shape of his head.
      The few trivial strands on top
      I leave them long. He is not bald.
           He limps into the bathroom
           and looks into the mirror.
      "It's so short," he rubs his head.
           "You won't have to cut it
           for another three months," I shout.
      He smiles with his lips together
      not wanting to show the gaps inside his mouth.
               Am I there yet?
急尿嗎?   屙屎嗎? 屙禁多尿又唔肯著尿片   Turn on the light.
        We've never imagined that the years would change us.
(in Mandarin) 今天不好. 我很累. 謝謝你們來看我.   It's dark here.
          喂, 點解佢忽然間講起國語禁奇怪?   Am I there yet
          Open the door.   I'm sick
          Am I there yet?   and you don't even know it.

·
·

(Hong Kong, 1967)
You brought home a surprise
knowing that we would never object to such a beauty.
While attending the symphony at City Hall
you were struck by her voice, rich and plaintive at the same time.
She came back in a large, heavy leather case.
We watched as you balanced her protuberance between your knees
one hand on her long, slender neck
the other hand gliding a bow across her silvery hair.
You learned to coax--sometimes gentle, sometimes forceful
and her reaction was immediate and honest,
letting you know if you touched her correctly.
The curiosity about this new love was unbounded,
so that at times I found the cello lying on her back on the dining room table
her four strings loosened from the tail piece, dangling backward on the pegs.
With the ceiling lamp pulled close, scalding the top of your head,
you rubbed the feet of the bridge back and forth
on a piece of sand paper you placed over her belly.
Other times you dwelled on a single note playing it over and over
until you were satisfied with the tone.
      "Turn on the light
The continuous utterance of the cello traveled down the hallway,
      it's dark here.
weaving in and out of rooms as I did my homework,
      I'm sick
talked on the phone, and went to sleep.
      and you don't even know it."
I was comforted knowing that you were here.

·
·

Take my staff , plant it in the sand
wash it with salt of the sea
deck the nodes with weeds
in the land of frankincense and myrrh.

Notes:

My father is suffering from dementia as I write this poem. We have hired a wonderful Chinese caretaker who speaks only his native Toyshan dialect. Our daily communication is confined to the immediate needs of my father, as my understanding of this dialect is extremely limited.

Translation of the Chinese character lines:

> Good morning, Mr. Ma. How are you?
> Don't get up yourself. Let me help you. Otherwise you'll fall again.
> Old folks need to drink more soup. Mr. Ma, drink more soup.
> He gets up after sleeping for no more than ten minutes, then walks in and out nonstop.
> He has eaten up everything. Isn't that so?

Last three lines in Chinese:

Caregiver in Toyshan—You want to pee? Want to crap? Pee so much but won't put on a diaper.

Father in Mandarin—Today, no good. I'm tired. Thank you for coming.

Daughter in Cantonese—Hey, strange that he is suddenly speaking in Mandarin.

Sweet Monday

Each day should be as sweet as Monday
to think of my love and write a verse
with a kiss
and I can tell
all is not sad
when the heart is glad.

Are you glad
sweet Monday
can you not be made sad?
If I come up with a bad verse
pray, do not tell
and I shall bribe you with a kiss.

But there is such a thing as a sour kiss
when my love is grumpy instead of glad
and if you wonder how anyone can tell
visit him on Friday instead of Monday
and he'll show you a crumpled verse
full of tears and sighs, ah… sad.

Days without love are sad
as are days without a kiss
but a poet who sells his soul for a verse
shall never be glad
and doesn't deserve a sweet Monday
as far as I can tell.

And who can tell
that my wild crazy lover is sad
waiting for his sweet Monday
pining for the kiss
and when Monday comes his world turns glad
writes a triolet for a verse.

A loving verse

breaking silence to tell
that his heart is glad
even when some of the days are sad
and as long as there is a kiss
the day's as lovely as sweet Monday.

I'm glad it's nearing the end of the verse
and soon sweet Monday will come, to tell
my sad eyes to close and wait for my lover's kiss.

Reunion

"How shall our conversation begin?"
Those sad eyes that came with youth are still sad after forty years.
"What's your fortune?"
He lacks color, a quality she finds boring.
But his hands, lascivious in nature
the heat of his palm penetrates her back.

The waiter comes back
suggests spicy shrimp with chili sauce to begin.
But he's Cantonese, mild in nature.
The hot in his throat won't spice up the years.
Each kernel of rice, boring.
He wants to know her fortune.

There is no fortune.
Her laughter is like a whip that cracks his back.
Anything conventional is boring.
Adventures begin
when she tosses away the obedient years
and goes wild with her nature.

Sad is his nature
no stomach for a cookie's fortune.
Lost are the precious years
of love that has turned its back.
How did it begin
and how did it end up so boring?

She smiles at the word "boring."
Her pepper gray hair, a token of nature.
Sand and camels begin
her journey. Fortune
is the long yellow scarf draped on her back
as she walks through the years.

He probes, as if to bring her back from those years

to God's sanctuary, which she finds boring,
to sit back
and reflect on her nature
her misguided fortune
and to begin

to repair the boring years
as nature finds ways to begin,
his warm hand, good fortune on her back.

New Year

At the stroke of midnight
>   *We are the Magi*
we cross over into a vast space
>   *arriving with gifts*
with objects unformed
>   *for that which we do not*
and names unknown
>   *understand*
only desire is made stronger
>   *Desire*
by the presence of a star
>   *leads us*
the same star
>   *and ignorant Love*
that has been guiding us
>   *We are the unknowing*
since all the forgotten years.
>   *monarchs of nothing*
It is bright in the new night
>   *arriving in the morning*
ever enchanting
>   *of the New*
we have far to go
>   *We have far to go*
and much to do.
>   *Magic drives us.*

—Clara Hsu / *Jack Foley*

THE FOOL

About the Author

Clara Hsu practices the art of multi-dimensional being: mother, musician, purveyor of Clarion Music Center (1982-2005), traveler, translator and poet.

A nominee for the Pushcart Prize in poetry (2001), Clara's first book of poems, *Mystique*, received honorable mention at the 2010 San Francisco Book Festival. A book of short stories, *Babouche Impromptu and Other Moroccan sketches* was completed in 2008 and published by Poetry Hotel Press. Her work can be found in *New Millennium Writings* (2012), *Hafenklänge, Havenklanken—Sounds of Harbor* (translations of her work into Dutch and German), *The Haight-Ashbury Literary Journal*, and the internet journals *Cha, The Other Voices International Project,* and *Tower Journal.* She was the featured poet in the 33rd issue of the British poetry journal, *erbacce.*

Clara gives featured readings at various Bay Area venues and benefit events, often in collaboration with others such as Bill Mercer and Jack and Adelle Foley. Her activities include her unusual performance ensemble "Lunation," which combines Chinese and original poetry with Asian traditional instruments. For seven years she hosted the Poetry Hotel Salon in San Francisco and with John Rhodes she co-hosts the San Francisco Open Mic Poetry Podcast TV Show. With Jack Foley she co-edits Poetry Hotel Press.

Visit: clarahsu.com

Author's photo by Bob Fischer.

Notes

Made in the USA
San Bernardino, CA
29 July 2014